Rom like Thunder

Hedina Tahirović Sijerčić

ROM LIKE THUNDER

Translated by Iva Berleković

MAGORIA BOOKS
Toronto, 2013

Hedina Tahirović Sijerčić & Derviš Alija Tahirović

Confession

This story began long ago, when I was a student and my father was still in his prime.

My father didn't spend a long time in school, nor had he gained any academic experience later in life. He did have an abundance of life experience to compensate; but I don't believe that life is the best teacher. It certainly hadn't been for him. Derviš Tahirović, my father, earned his bread and fed our family by working as a taxi driver during the day, and occasionally even at night.

My father's lifetime of labour in several different trades made his hands too rough for writing. Before I started school, he worked for a company called "Metalotehna" in Skenderija. Then he decided to become his own boss and purchased a Praga truck, using it to do deliveries. This Praga was an old vehicle that broke down constantly; but he somehow always fixed it and generally maintained it with love, knowing it would continue to provide a good income. Then later, once it had broken down completely, he purchased a small Fiat truck for a replacement. He had also built a garage next to our house where he used to fix his friends' cars, to get some more money coming in.

Eventually, he managed to save enough money to purchase a car, which he then used to become a taxi driver. But his love for blacksmithing, a trade he learned from his father, never left him. After working as a taxi driver for some time, he set up a workshop in his garage, and constructed a utility trailer using materials cut and welded by himself. Soon news of my father's abilities started spreading among his colleagues, who began to order trailers of their own from him, because they saw that his work was good enough to pass even official traffic inspections.

He called himself "Rom like Thunder", and the description fit. His hands knew how to make small gifts for us children. From metal, he would cut stars, moons, and circles for decorating our Christmas tree. I also remember galloping horses, which he made out of wire.

He was a tireless and hardworking man, my father.

Rom like Thunder

"I wish somebody would write this story of mine to preserve it. My journals and memories, I leave to my children: Jasminka, Hedina, Alma, Ehlimana, Elvira, and Alin. May they pass them on to their children. Lest it be forgotten."

"Sit down, my son Dinda, and write!"

How many times in my childhood did I hear these words... "Dinda" was my father's affectionate name for me. And he called me "son" instead of "daughter", as that was the common term of endearment for both sons and daughters.

My father was in one of his special moods on the day he asked me to write his memoirs about his family. Since he was not skilled at writing, he would dictate, and I, his child, would write down his stories in his stead. Yet I always had to be extremely patient until he was finally ready to speak.

I can still picture it in my mind: my father sitting at the edge of his bed, next to him a small chair, on the chair a pot, and atop the pot a plate with finger food, a carafe, and a shot glass filled with brandy.

"Write, Dinda," my father would say, right before sinking back into his memories. He would become pensive, as his eyes—which always seemed so beautiful to me—grew misty, and his gaze wandered far away. I would look into those beautiful eyes to try to catch a glimpse of his soul. I wanted to see what he was seeing with his faraway gaze. He wanted something to be recorded. But what? How can one who is used only to short, scattered sentences instead of long conversations manage to write a story?

My father always spoke to us, his children, with his eyes. We learned from him that it would suffice to peer into each other's eyes to know what we had to do. Our conversations with our eyes were always something uniquely ours. Our lips were sealed in silence, but our eyes were talking. To others, these were just passing glances; yet to our family, they were secret conversations, whose meanings no outsider could guess. Our father and we—his daughters and his son—all knew the meaning of every shimmer and every spark in each other's eyes.

"Are you writing, Dinda?" my father would always ask.

"Yes, Tata, I am writing." I would answer.

Other children in the neighbourhood called their fathers "Babo", but we always called ours "Tata". I don't know why. Perhaps he once told his eldest daughter to call him that, and it became our tradition. This made us special. This made us different. But it was not easy to be different in our neighbourhood. Even our cousins teased us over our saying"Tata", and even more because of our skin colour, which was lighter than theirs. Jealous with envy, they teased us by calling us ladies, "the Ladies Tahirović". And yet, we didn't feel like ladies, nor any different because of our fair skin. We were the same as our father, just Roma from Gorica.

"Write, Dinda", demanded my father whenever this special mood would hit him. "Lest it be forgotten how we once lived, how we now live in the Romani *mahala* of Gorica."

*   *   *

Our mother Dragica isn't a Romani woman. She didn't understand my father's "lest it be forgotten", because she wanted to forget everything about her childhood and her youth.

Mother was born and raised in another part of Sarajevo, Marijin Dvor at the centre of the city. She was Catholic by birth, and had acquired a curious nickname through her baptism. The priest performing the ceremony was called Gagula, and children who knew her had named her after him. Our father was one of the few people who knew that nickname of hers. Very rarely would my mother talk about her childhood, as she preferred to try to forget.

Her father Andrija had been a butcher by trade, and a brutish and uneducated man. He drank a lot, and gravely harassed his wife, my grandmother Ankica, who suffered for many years before she finally summoned up the courage to leave her husband, and when she did she left her children too.

Soon after that my grandparents divorced, and my grandfather brought home another woman by the name of name of Hasnija, who only worsened the misery of my mother's childhood. Hasnija was a stepmother right out of a cruel fairy tale. But at least, she wasn't to be my grandfather's last wife. Years later, he married a Hungarian woman, Marija, with whom he eventually grew old.

My mother had always considered her youngest sister, Mirjana, to be her most fortunate sibling, as she lived with grandfather's sister, Ikica, while growing up. As for the rest of them, my grandfather wanted to pass on his butcher's trade to his daughters. He had worked in the slaughterhouse, and that is where my mother and her sister Zdenka had to work also, to learn everything about making sausages. This allowed him to watch over them constantly.

Dragica, Dinda (Hedina), and Derviš Tahirović

Mother didn't have anything nice to say about her father or the childhood she spent with him. Sometimes, she would sit among us children, pulling her long thick hair into a pony-tail, and she would say with a sigh: "When we were small, father used to cut our hair with a knife."

She couldn't add another word. Her face would go into a spasm, as if she was reliving the memory of her father cutting her hair with a knife. She would stay silent for several minutes. In my mind, I could see every movement of the knife cutting my mother's hair; and each tear my mother had shed during these occasions.

Then suddenly, she would sigh aloud before adding: "We had to wear deep rubber boots. It was awful. All the other children wore beautiful shoes and leather boots in the winter; only we wore deep, men's rubber boots. Father wouldn't allow long hair either. He would order a hairdresser to make us perms. That's the way he thought it proper for young ladies."

* * *

When mother spoke of those times, I thought about how these black boots were passed on to our generation as well. In the fall, mother and father would buy us rubber boots also, as they were better suited than anything else to our *mahala*'s mud; mostly because they would keep our feet dry, but also because they could always be washed.

We wore those same boots to school, and would wash off the mud stuck to our heels and soles every day at the faucet behind the old Zejlaginca house at the bottom of the street. After washing off the mud, our shiny black boots would emerge. We would then summon the courage to walk with our clean boots towards Gorica street.

On our way to school, a family of non-Roma, who had only recently moved to Gorica, would wait for us on this street. Their children would kick us, and spit on us: "Cigani! Cigani! You bloody cigani, you cannot pass here!" Their parents would laugh at us, encouraging their children's abusive behaviour. But we were always ready to defend ourselves. From our deep, wide rubber boots, we would pull out rocks, and throw them at our tormentors. This was our daily battle on our way to school.

Mother would often accompany us to school to protect us from these miscreants waiting for us on the lower street. She undertook this task boldly, and would escort us to school and protect us as much as she could, without telling father about our troubles. She knew that he had an abrupt temper, and that he would go down to fight with those people if he heard about what went on day after day. And this, of course, would mean that *all the men* in our *mahala* would join in the fight. It would be a war between the Roma and the newcomers, and my mother didn't want that.

At least in school, we didn't stand out from the other children. Like our classmates, we had lockers for shoes and coats. We would take off our rubber boots and put on black slippers.

Although father earned a good living, there was never enough money for new clothing. We wore a lot of hand-me-downs that our mother would buy from our grandmother Mejra, who got them by begging throughout the city. But nice clothes were often given to us by grandma Ankica, who cleaned in wealthier households, and who was given clothing that didn't fit her employers' children. Yes, one could wear these clothes; they were almost always beautiful and modern. We always eagerly awaited grandma Ankica with her full bags.

Of course, it didn't really matter what we wore since we would cover our often worn out, but clean clothing with the same school apron that all students had to wear. All the same, it was always in the beginning of the school year that we would get new clothing.

We didn't have new school books. Mother would make a list of books for each of her daughters, and then take us to some book booths on Koševo street, where she would buy used books. New books, and school supplies were far too expensive. Father didn't allow the school, and other social institutions to give us any "gratis books", as he called them.

"I am still alive, I will buy everything for you." he would explain. "I am capable of feeding you and providing for your schooling. You are not orphans. My children don't need gratis books or social assistance."

"You are not like other Roma, and neither am I," my father would tell us at the beginning of each school year. But the notebooks and school supplies always had to be new, so mother would buy them at the bookstore "Veselin Masleša" in Marijin Dvor. I will never forget the smell of new notebooks, and the natural scent of wood from which paper was made. As soon as I held them in my hands, I would smell them, taking in a deep breath; the smell of new and clean...

Often, I would place my notebooks under my pillow because I found the scent so pleasant. As a child who believed in miracles, I imagined that the notebooks and books I placed under my pillow had special powers, and that knowledge from them would flow straight into my mind.

I pretended that the first of every month was the beginning of a new school year, and the scent of new notebooks always awakened my thirst for knowledge.

                    *   *   *

When mother was in good spirits, she would recount some mystical happenings from her youth. She lived with her father in a house next to the Magribija mosque at the Marijin Dvor. My mother would recall our grandpa Andrija's heavy drinking and general fearlessness. Even though he was Catholic, he socialized a lot with the Roma. He even learned a few words of Romani. For example he would often use the expression "Ma dara" which means, "Do not be afraid". His friend

Alija Sarajlija had taught him this. Such short anecdotes between reality and fiction seemed to make my mother's life more beautiful for a moment.

"At midnight we could hear the banging of pots in the cabinet." she recalled. "It was so loud that Zdenka and I feared we might go deaf. We covered our ears with our hands and trembled in horror. We gathered on the bed and our father gently told us, 'Ma dara. Calm down, don't be afraid! It will pass. Now let me show you something.' Then he got up and opened the doors leading to the hallway, 'Listen to this now. Come here and take a look.'

"We heard somebody walking through the hallway and when we approached our father, we saw two empty boots marching through the hallway. We couldn't believe our eyes: there were no legs in them! We saw each stride and listened to each step. At that moment, father approached the cabinet and opened all the doors. Pot covers were jumping up and down and made a deafening thumping noise. He would tell us quietly: 'Watch now, once midnight comes everything will finish and the thumping will stop.' We waited.

"All of a sudden the room got quiet. We looked at the clock. At five minutes past midnight, the boots stopped marching and the pot covers stopped rattling. 'Ma dara children, we are close to the mosque and graves. It is the good that get up at night. They won't harm you. Don't ever fear the dead, fear the living instead.'"

Mother would tell us that her father was right, as he himself was to be feared more than the spirits of the dead that visited at night. No wonder my mother shared so few of her memories with us... most of them were so painful. Dragica Vrebac Tahirović desired only to forget her memories.

*   *   *

My father, Derviš Tahirović, on the other hand, wanted to remember his past and preserve his memories in writing. Why did Father want to remember? Even though my father didn't spend much time in school, he saw and felt the world around him. He sensed that it was important for our people to start leaving behind written traces of their lives.

Mina (Jasminka) in 1966.

Dinda (Hedina) in 1967.

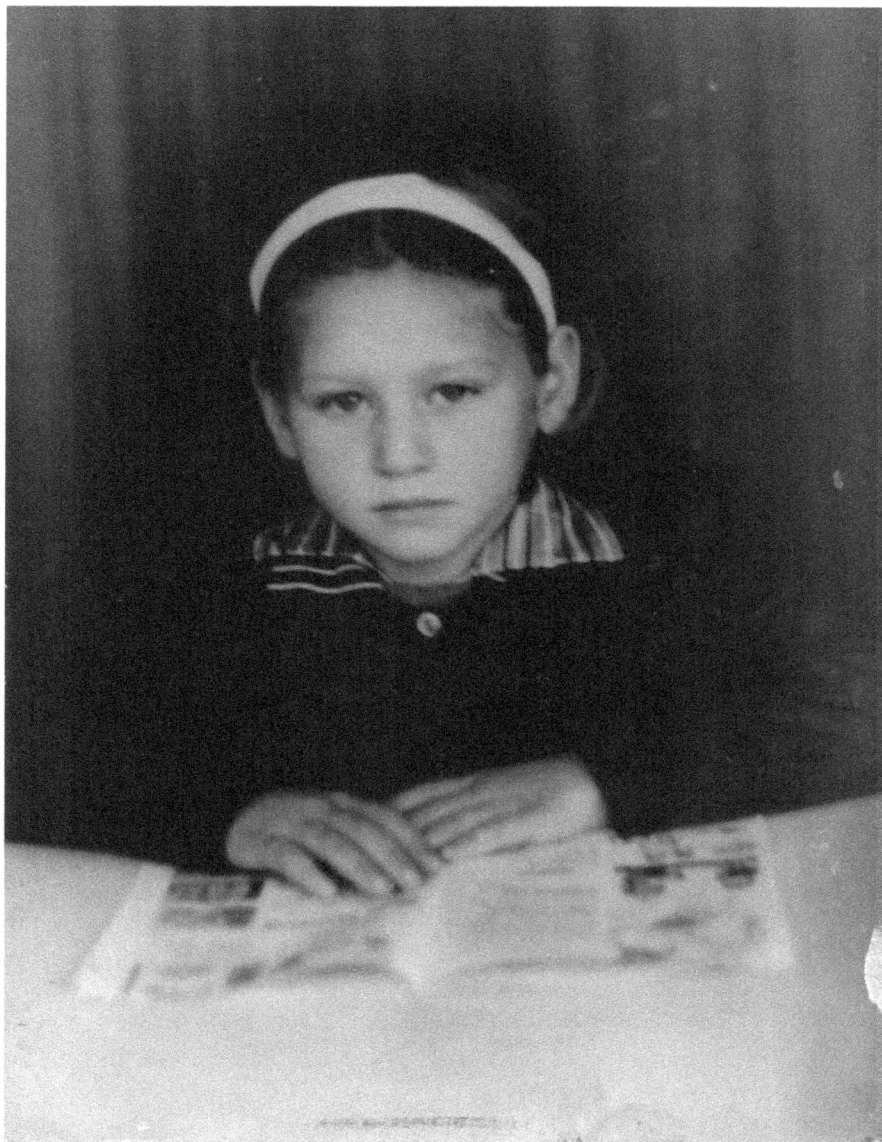

Baćo (Alma) in 1970.

Nana (Ehlimana) in 1972.

Lila (Elvira) in 1975.

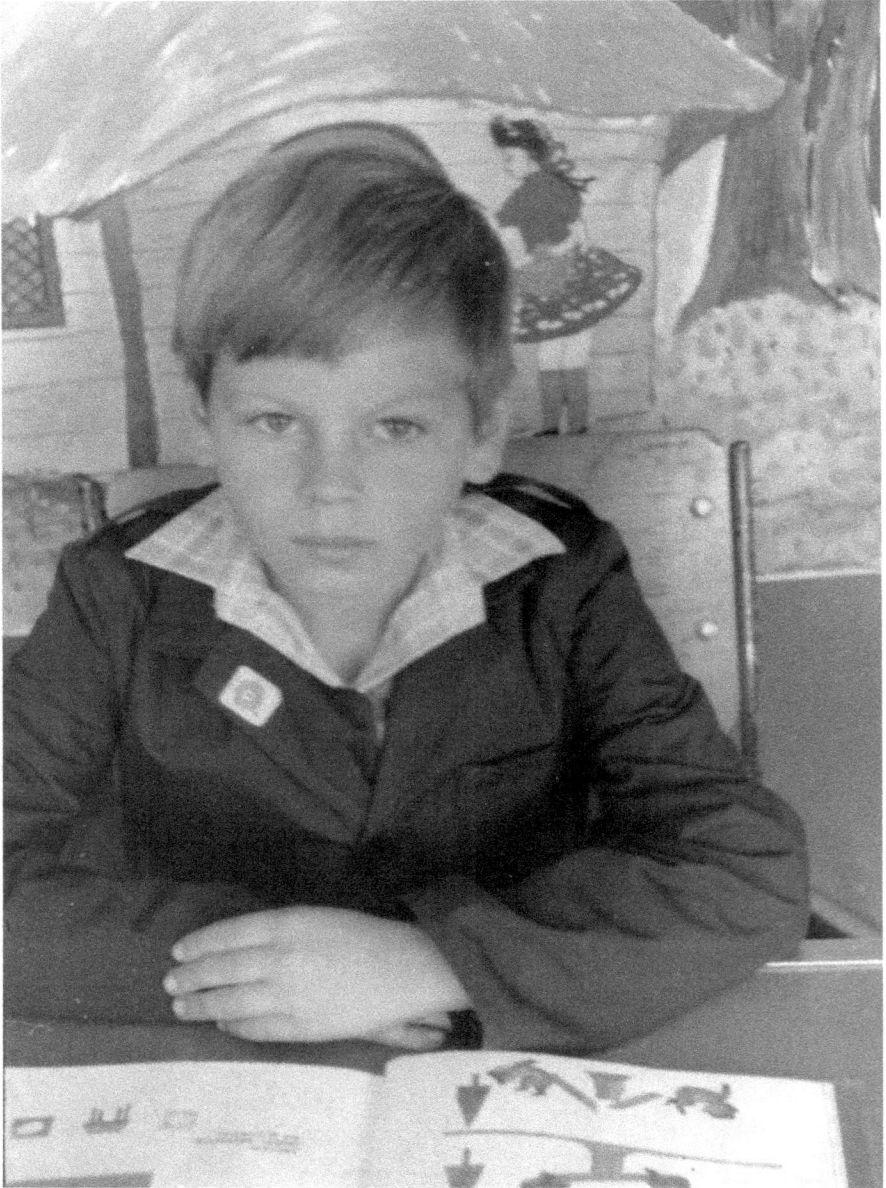

Aljo (Alin) in 1982.

There were difficulties with these confessions though. My father's wish to talk about his people was always the strongest when he was "in ćejf", that wisftful state of mild intoxication after a few drinks. And I, prepared with my special notebook, would wait and really wish for him to start talking already. I could sense his weariness at being unable to express his thoughts.

The story burned inside him, and he wanted it to emerge as something beautiful. But he just kept repeating the same phrases every time we sat down together to write. He wanted to rely on my literacy as a bright student, but forgot that I was just a 10 year old child who didn't understand much about the world.

I would try to peer into his eyes for clues, but even that didn't help. "It's so our Romani roots aren't swept away, and our heritage isn't forgotten," he would often explain. But all too often it seemed like I didn't understand what my father was trying to say, and so we would go over my notes anew.

I was born in our Romani mahala on April 16, 1940.

My father's house was a small single room shack, covered with a roof. It was located in Gorica, in the heart of Sarajevo on Crni Vrh, the Black Peak. Gorica is right next to Marijin Dvor, which includes the Railway station Velešići, the Stadium Koševo, Đuro Đaković street, a Central Committee office, a Military Hospital, and the movie theaters Kinoteka, Prvi Maj, Radnik, and Sutjeska. One can see the whole of Marijin Dvor from the mountain in Gorica.

I was born to Alija Tahirović (1893-1962), my father, and Merja Tahirović née Beganović (1912-1962), my mother. My paternal grandfather was called Derviš, just like me, and his wife, my paternal grandmother, was called Haska.

My maternal grandfather was called Salko Beganović. His family was originally nomadic, and travelled from place to place by horse carriage. In time, they tired of nomadic life, and settled down. My mother would often reminisce about how her family lived in Hadžići. She never told us where exactly, but her family had owned a house along with several acres of land and uncleared forest. During World War II, many of our people were executed simply for being Roma. The Fascists wanted to exterminate us all. The Ustaše killed my mother's parents, Hanija and Salko, all of her brothers, and most of her sisters. Their house had been burnt down, and everything in it had been

*Grandfather Alija's grave at the cemetery at Širokača, 1962. His sons Ramo
and Derviš stand at the front, with feses on their heads.*

lost. Only my mother Mejra and my aunt Umija had survived.

*Both sisters eventually married and had children. Umija gave birth
to three children: my cousin Džemo Pašić, and his two sisters, Mina and
Džemila. Džemo now lives with his wife Hiba, and has three children. Mina
married Ramiz. And her younger sister Džemila married a man called Safet.*

*Though Džemila's husband, Safet, was not a Rom, she still visited us
regularly in Gorica. Even now she maintains her family ties to us, because
she is not ashamed of her Romani ancestry, like so many others who left our
mahala. Džemila is a kind woman, a good friend, and my well-loved cousin.
She always has a smile on her face. She always looks so happy, but perhaps
she is only happy when visiting us here in Gorica. We always were her world,
it seems to me.*

*There is truth in this, my son. I felt it myself. We too once moved away
from our mahala. I had sold the house, and we moved into an apartment on
Vraca. We lived there for a while, but about it was difficult for me without
Gorica and our fellow Roma. It was hard for you also, my children; you didn't
have the freedom to go outside and play, and neither did you have friends
close by. Instead you were always confined to the apartment.*

Derviš Tahirović and Šerif Beganović

And so it was only a matter of time before we moved back to our old house. I had to buy it back for much more than I had sold it. One cannot exist without one's own kind, and Gorica is both my hapiness and my destiny. . . But let me finish the story about my mother Mejra and her sister Umija.

They were fortunate; for after having their whole family killed and finding themselves orphans without close relatives, my mother's cousin, Dervo Beganović, took them into his home and cared for them well.

Dervo was also the father of my cousin Šerif, my big "haver", as Sarajevans often call their best friend. Šerif is the only real haver I ever had in my life. He married Šuhra, a Muslim woman from Bijeljina.

Šerif had an older brother, Dervo, whose wife was called Agica. Neither brother had any children, but they did have many sisters. Unfortunately, as is often the case, after some years of marriage, both Šerif and Dervo left their wives and disappeared from the face of the earth as Roma too often do.

One of their sisters had a daughter called Vesna and a son called Džimi. Vesna now lives in Italy and Džimi had moved to Germany. Another sister,

Rabija, lived in Nova Gorica, at the border between Slovenia and Italy. She has children too. Šerif and I used to visit her often.

*   *   *

My father Alija, a blacksmith by trade, had his workshop on Koševsko brdo, exactly where the café Car was some years ago.

He was a hard-working man, my father. On most days, he worked all day long shoeing horses and making all kinds of trinkets on special order.

We were the four of us, me and my brothers: Ramo, the eldest, whom you kids call daidža; Ejub, the second eldest, whom we also call Mehmed and whom you call Stari; and I, Derviš, or Dedo to my nephews and nieces. And in our childhood, we had little time for games or for idly walking about Čaršija. We were always working with our father, who taught all four of us the blacksmithing trade early on.

And he didn't only teach us, but other boys in the neighbourhood as well. In fact, our Babo was a master craftsman with the right to keep apprentices and the authority to issue blacksmithing certificates to them.

In contrast, our two sisters, Zineta and Mubera, received neither education nor apprenticeship training, and became estranged once they had married. Especially Mubera.

I loved my parents very much. Babo was a quiet, calm man with a fair complexion and red cheeks. He always wore his red fes on his head—just like all real Sarajevan men back in those days.

And my mother... There are no longer women like her in this world. She was feisty and stern, and tall and slender, with a dark complexion, long black hair, and wide piercing eyes.

A courageous woman, always on her toes; she had the gift of healing and was especially good at removing badlje (what we nowadays call cataracts) from the eyes. Though she didn't charge for her services, she often received food, and even money from the people she healed.

She knew no fear... If only my daughters would take after her!

My parents loved and helped each other all their lives. My mother had died from grief a few months after my father had passed away. They are both buried in the Muslim graveyard on Širokača.

My Babo had two sisters, Šerifa and Ramiza, the latter of whom was sometimes called Ofajda. He also had two brothers, Mustafa and Mešan.

Babo was the second-born in his family. And my amidža Mešan was the strongest man in town.

When we spoke of my uncle, amidža Mešan, my father's face would light up. Not all Roma were miserable and frightened, at least not in my father's family. There were some, who could serve as example to others, like father's uncle Mešan. He was so strong and big enough that nobody dared to attack him. He wasn't poor either; he always had lots of money.

There used to be this big rock here in Gorica. It has since been removed, so I cannot show it to you. But it was enormous, and nobody could lift it! Amidža Mešan kept his money under that rock. He was the only one who could move that huge rock, so he never worried about having his money stolen. It was safer under that rock than it would have been even in his house. As a little boy, I had wanted to be as strong and as fearless as my amidža.

Father raised his shot glass in a toast to all these beautiful memories, then continued his story.

My parents only spoke Romani when they wanted to hide something from us children. You know yourselves that children can't keep a secret, and how they often tell the neighbors things they shouldn't tell. Our mother didn't teach us our Romani language, she taught us Bosnian instead. Such a pity! This is the reason that I couldn't teach you the Romani language either.

My brothers Ejub-Mehmed and Ramo know more Romani than I do, as they are older than I am. But though we might not know Romani, we are Roma, and we have our heritage. I was never ashamed of it! My children, I am Rom like Thunder. Don't ever forget that.

Others may call us different names: Cigani, Gypsies, Kalopers, Firauns, Chergars and other made-up derogatory names. Let them call us what they please, let them call us pots and pans; but never let them break us.

We are dark, but our souls are not. You see, my children, my cheeks look dark, after the complexion of our ancestors. But don't you, my children, ever do things to make it even darker. Be honest, children, and keep faith in the one and only God almighty.

As time goes by, more and more Romani families are arriving to Sarajevo. Šiptar people from Kosovo, Chergashi from Sandžak, Goražde, and Vlasenica. As more and more of them arrive, our Romani kin, my cousins and friends, withdraw from Romani circles and try to forget who they are, ashamed of their roots and their own dark complexion. They lose their pride and take on the shame of others.

The black markets and the begging of these newcomers drove us Sarajevan Roma from our own kind. "We are nothing like them!" our so-called white Roma of Sarajevo used to say, pulling ever further away from us. Eventually, not even wanting to acknowledge those of us who had stayed behind.

They were cutting themselves off from the Roma of Gorica. They were cutting themselves off from their culture, their traditions, and their identity. With time, they even stopped self-identifying with their nationality, and became Muslims instead. Not through their religious beliefs, but more on account of their Islamic names, given to us and our forefathers at birth.

They believed that Muslims would view them as equals. But I think they were mistaken. Rom is always Rom, this can neither be washed away, nor be erased from our čehra. Even in my family, many are estranged, wanting to be Muslims, Bošnjaks.

My pen rests on the paper. Is my father not a Muslim? He prays and sometimes teaches us suras from Qur'an. Just the other day, he called us to gather around him:

"Come now, Mina, Alma, and Lila. Take a pen and paper and write. That which you will write, you should memorize by heart, as it is from the Qur'an and you have to know it. Come! Write my children:

> Bismillahi rrahmani rrahim.
> El hamdu lillahi,
> Rabbil'alemin,
> Errahmani rrahim,
> Maliki jevmiddin.
> Ijjake na'budu,
> Ve ijjake neste'in,
> Ihdine ssiratal mustekim,
> Siratallezine en'amte'alejhim.
> Gajril magdobi'alejhim,
> Vele ddallin-Amin!

Amin!

"This, my children, means:

> "In the name of Allah, the Beneficent, the Merciful.
> All praise is due to Allah,
> The Lord of the Worlds,
> The Beneficent, the Merciful,

Master of the Day of Judgment.
Thee do we serve,
And Thee do we beseech for help,
Keep us on the right path,
The path of those upon whom Thou hast bestowed favors.
Not of those upon whom Thy wrath is brought down,
Nor of those who go astray!

Amen!

"Let us now repeat this prayer all together. Read out for me what you have written down, and be sure to memorize it later."

I wrote down what my father had dictated, but I didn't understand a word of it. He said that we shouldn't become estranged from our Romani heritage, as we will never be accepted as Bosnians or Muslims, he also regularly taught us from the Qur'an, and even buried his cousin, our daidža Rašid, according to Muslim custom.

*   *   *

Why did we call our uncle Rašid *daidža*, mother's brother, when he was our uncle from father's side? I do not know. But perhaps it was because he had been written off by his relatives, and expelled from his family's home on account of his heavy drinking. He had never married and never had any children. Alcohol destroyed him early on in his youth.

My father always tried to help his relatives when they were in trouble, and daidža Rašid was no exception. I remember him as a good man, who never hurt anyone. Also seeing this goodness, my father let him stay with us, turning our basement into an apartment to provide shelter for him.

Daidža was the very stereotype of a Rom from Gorica. He was short, dark skinned, with dark shiny hair combed over his head. He always wore light shirts with jersey pants, and a jacket. Such attire was traditional, and was worn by most men of the Tahirović family for generations, and also by Sarajevan Roma in general.

Daidža Rašid was very child-like in his own way. He was always eager to fulfill my wishes, often carrying me piggy-back, "krkače", while running down Turbe towards the Railway Station, while I rocked on his back and shouted "Go horse, go!". He would even neigh and whinny like a horse for my amusement, because he enjoyed this child's game. We would both laugh and feel happy. We never returned home right away, as he always stopped to have a brandy in one of the pubs at the station, and then somewhere else to get a chocolate for me. Afterwards, he would again carry me krkače and climb up Turbe back to Gorica. But it wasn't in our destiny to play together for much longer.

The fact that Daidža was never sick and never complained about any pains made it all the stranger that moved into ahiret, the other world, so suddenly. One afternoon, as I was sitting with my sister Jasminka on the balcony of our house, daidža Rašid was walking under the balcony, and he wobbled on his feet, left foot crossing the right, right crossing the left. My sister and I were laughing our hearts out, thinking that daidža was, as always, playing with us. We believed that he was walking like a clown to make us laugh. But he didn't look at us, and he didn't even hear our laughter as he passed us by.

Going down the stairs leading to his apartment in the basement, he tottered and fell, even as we still laughed. We called, his name, but he didn't respond, and he didn't get up either. Only in that moment, did we finally understand that something horrible had happened, and we started to scream.

Our mother and several of our neighbors came running, and tried to help him. But white foam was already coming from his mouth. Everybody yelled: "He's dead. He's dead." One calm voice said: "Rahmet, blessed be his soul," as is customary in Muslim families.

We stopped screaming, though our eyes remained wide open from the shock of seeing our daidža's motionless body on the ground, still having thought, that he was playing with us just moments ago. I didn't know why, but our mother ordered us to leave the house. Nura, an elderly neighbor, arrived and took us to her veranda. The only thing I remember afterwards is that they took daidža Rašid into the house, and placed him onto the bed. He was dead.

My father wanted me to record in the notebook the memory of his cousin's death. As he was speaking, his tears became welled up, and my eyes became watery as well, because I loved that man dearly as a child.

"Are you writing, my son?"

Daidža Rašid was prepared for the funeral according to both Muslim customs and our own traditions. Men washed him and wrapped him into a white bedsheet, while our mother covered the television and all the mirrors in the house with tablecloths and kerchiefs. It was believed that the reflection of the deceased in the mirror could bring misfortune. Then we opened the window slightly, and placed a pot with water on the window sill. If the deceased died thirsty, his soul, still around the house, could come and have a last drink. And if he died hungry? According to the custom, we poured some flour into a plate and placed it onto the window sill, next to the water, so that his soul would have something to eat. We flattened the flour with the paper, convinced that his soul, as light as it might be, would still leave traces, which would be easier to spot on the smoothed surface of the flour. It was recounted in the families who have lost their members that after some time one half of the water disappears and that fingerprints are left on the flour surface. According to these accounts, for some time after the death, the souls of the deceased linger for their last meal, their nafaka. Who knows how much of this was true...

Daidža Rašid was prepared for the funeral according to both Muslim customs and our own traditions. Men washed him and wrapped him into a white bedsheet, while our mother covered the television and all the mirrors in the house with tablecloths and kerchiefs. It was believed that the reflection of the deceased in the mirror could bring misfortune. Then we opened the window slightly, and placed a pot with water on the window sill. If the deceased died thirsty, his soul, still around the house, could come and have a last drink. And if he died hungry? According to the custom, we poured some flour into a plate and placed it onto the window sill, next to the water, so that his soul would have something to eat. We flattened the flour with the paper, convinced that his soul, as light as it might be, would still leave traces, which would be easier to spot on the smoothed surface of the flour. It was recounted in the families who have lost their members that after some time one half of the water disappears and that fingerprints are left on the flour surface. According to these accounts, for some time after the death, the souls of the deceased linger for their last meal, their nafaka. Who knows how much of this was true...

According to the custom, men kept an all night vigil beside the deceased , as this was their way of parting from him. Everybody wanted the deceased to pardon them for one thing or another, or to recount an anecdote from his life, and or simply to honour their friendship with Rašid. At the same time, women were gathered in a separate room, bowing and praying for the soul of the deceased. We had, of course, informed the doctor who had the task of determining the cause of death. We also made arrangements with a funeral home to organize the burial. After at least twenty four hours, as tradition prescribed, the morgue's wagon arrived to our mahala *to take him away. As always, everybody in the* mahala *came out of their houses and stood in front of their doors with buckets full of water in their hands. As the morgue's wagon was leaving, everybody poured water from their buckets and the water flew downhill. Empty buckets were turned upside down and left on the street for some time. The* mahala *and the Roma were sending the deceased off with the words, "Go with the God, go with the water. Dza Devleh(s)a, dza pajeh(s)a."*

We didn't forget our Romani creeds, either. We were always careful that there was no animal in the vicinity while the deceased was still in the house, or even while he was carried out to the wagon. An animal could cut off his path to the other world. The elders believed that the soul of a deceased could enter into the body of an animal, which would be a grave misfortune for the family. And let's not forget that only men could attend burials. After which, it was imperative to wash one's hands and shoes before leaving the graveyard.

Once the burial was over, everyone would gather in the house of the deceased. There, the people who attended the funeral would be offered food and served coffee. Women had two tasks, cooking and serving the visitors, and praying tevhide, *for the deceased person's soul and salvation, with the help of the* Bula, *the enlightened woman.*

Remember my son, you should never go to your own house after the funeral, as that will cause great troubles.

We had many a happy childhood moment with poor Rašid. And we sent him off to his death laughing.

*   *   *

My father had many more stories about less fortunate relatives from Gorica, and the role that alcohol played in their misfortune.

"Are you writing, Dinda? Who will we write about now?" continued my father, taking a sip of brandy. "What about my aunt Šerifa? She merits that something about her be recorded."

Derviš and Ramo carry a relative's coffin

I looked at him and nodded, as I also thought that my aunt was a dear woman who deserved to be remembered. He, in turn, peeked into my notebook and glanced over my writing, then nodded and looked at me with tenderness. He was obviously pleased with what he saw, and continued his dictation.

Aunt Šerifa, my father's sister, lived right by our house. She was a tiny woman, and old age creased her face with wrinkles. Then again, perhaps it wasn't old age, but rather life that had carved those wrinkles. She covered her long, grey, braided hair with a white šamija. *She always wore nice clean dresses, and a lovely* kat.

My father paused, looked at me as if wanting to confirm that I knew what he was talking about. I blinked to signal that I did. "Of course, I know." I answered silently in my mind. A kat *is that beautiful combination of a blouse and a* dimije, *worn by Muslim women within the home.*

It was also worn by our women. In the afternoon, we could always see our Aunt Šerifa in front of her house. She would get out and walk around, waiting for her son R— to come home from work. She worried a lot about him. He was always on her mind whenever she cleaned her house or whitewashed its walls.

My aunt worked hard, even doing the most difficult chores on her own. As she swept the road in front of her house, she would firmly clinch her broom with her small, frail hands with puffed up veins. Hunched in this manner, she managed to look even smaller, casting a shadow looking more like that of a child.

Her son R— never made her happy with anything. He drank a lot, and while drunk, he would abuse his wife F—, the mother of two daughters: A— and H—. We would hear his drunken howls from our house.

"What is it, F—, why did you rush into the house?" R— would yell from the street. His wife would run out over to the doorstep and stand petrified in fear, waiting for his raised arm to strike her in the head. "I am over here, R—. I am coming, I was cooking lunch. I'm coming." She would lean down to untie his shoelaces before leading him into the house, but even as she was bent over, he would kick her as if she was a football.

Our Romani women learned from their parents to respect their husbands no matter what, even accepting this behavior. You lean down to take his shoes off, even if he kicks you while you do it. This is the model of Romani woman in Gorica! Our parents taught us that the humbler a woman was, the harder she would get hit. But the less humble ones, who resisted would also get beaten. We were taught that a woman is a lesser being that deserves to be hit. This is how it has been in our Romani families for many centuries, to let it be known that it is the man who rules the house.

F— tolerated this mistreatment for a very long time, because aunt Šerifa was looking after her, though they both lived in constant fear of being beaten. F— had found work in the city, and the money she earned she used to better support her family. After work, she would always be waiting for her drunken husband, forever fearful of what he might come up with next. And he always came up with a reason to beat her.

After aunt Šerifa passed away, his drinking, and violent behavior towards her had become unbearable. F— took her children and moved out of Gorica. She had left R—, being unable to tolerate his abuse any longer, and R— died from alcohol abuse, alone, and abandoned.

My father, while talking about his cousin, who beat his wife and died from alcohol abuse, would pause between sentences to sip from his shot glass. He would be in a state of *ćejf*, and his mind would wander. He would take a moment to pause, think, then bang his shot glass against the table. Then with *merak*, he would take another sip of brandy, followed by another bite of food.

"Dinda, do you remember our R— and E—?"

Yes, I remember them. This was the man who beat his wife in front of everyone: children, family members, neighbors. He would kick her, and hit her in the back and head. Everyone would watch silently, without ever defending the poor woman, as if they were waiting to see if he would finally kill her. When someone would finally reach the point where they couldn't watch their scene anymore, people would physically separate the couple, and take R— to a bar for a brandy to appease him. But he never stayed appeased for long.

The ambulance would arrive and take E— to the hospital to stop the bleeding and sew her up, while R— was drinking from his *šiša*. While drunk, he would sit on the ground next to the fence, with his shirt unbuttoned, and his hair messy. He would drink directly from his *šiša*. Then, once the bottle was empty, he would smash it on his own head until it broke into pieces. Blood would pour down his head, and feeling small and nasty, he would threaten everybody with pieces of broken glass—no one would dare to approach him.

While in this state of alcohol-induced delirium, he would eat broken glass. Blood would pour down his mouth, travelling down his chin and tainting his shirt. This scene was horrifying for us children to watch. At some point, he would fall asleep and would continue to just lie there until his family would take him home.

This destructive habit impacted so many families in our *mahala* of Gorica. Alcoholism was frequent among our men, and even among some of our women. While R— was beating his wife, other Roma would sit nearby in a circle, playing a game of dice called *barbut*. Others would move around and watch for police patrols.

The police was always in or around our *mahala*. When people would notice policemen, they would yell "Ake tele pačardo", "The police is coming!", and all the players would quickly gather their money and dice, and disappear. When our people were gambling, they didn't care who was winning or what was happening around them. This too was typical for *mahalas* in Sarajevo.

Was this also something that my father didn't want forgotten? Everyone seemed to reenact the same patterns of behavior: Husbands and fathers would drink, sleep with prostitutes, and beat their wives; whereas women would suffer in silence; and their children would watch and remember.

I wanted to believe that my father was different, even though he also drank. But unlike other men, he reminisced about the past while in a state of *ćejf* and remained good to us. He would always share his *meze*, with us children. He would bring a piece of meat to my mouth with his fork, telling me, "Eat, my son!"

My dear father, he never wanted to eat alone. He would gather his children around the table, and would feed us with his fork or spoon. Mother would soon get angry, feeling that we were bothering our father, who should have been allowed to eat in peace. Father would then tenderly call her by her nickname, Gagula: "Let them be, Gagula. Let them be. They're not bothering me at all. Let the children be near me." He would then continue to share his food with each one of us in turn.

These were rare, lovely moments in my family. I understood that when my father called my mother "Gagula", it meant that he loved her in those moments. He would speak in a soothing voice, as if caressing her. I remember these times fondly.

*   *   *

Though my father was always working, and made lots of money that he always brought home, he and my mother were rarely smiling or in good spirit. These were loving moments in my family. In my heart, I knew that when my father would affectionaly call my mother, Gagula, it meant that he loved her in those moments. He would utter her name in a soothing voice, as if it were a caress. This was usually followed by moments of peace in our house.

Even though my father was constantly working, and made a lot of money, which he always brought home, rare were those moments when our mother was in a good spirit and smiling. I believed that our father's *fes* was always full of money. He always bought my mother presents in an attempt to make her happy, and to lift her spirits. He often bought gold jewelry. She must have owned more than a kilogram of gold, and his *fes* was always loaded with money. Her face would light up in delight as soon as she saw it. Those times she wouldn't even mind if father had too much to drink. She would take the *fes* into her hands, and count the money. She would sometimes count and recount the same pile of money ten times or more, while claiming that she made an error and the total wasn't adding up correctly.

Though I was just a child then, I realized how much my mother enjoyed having money in her hands. This was a pleasure that both my parents shared. He enjoyed money, and was proud to bring my mother lots of of it, and she secretly enjoyed having my father watching her lovingly count the bills. These were moments that my mother wanted to hold onto for as long as possible.

I would glance at my mother, trying to understand what all the fuss was about—she already knew how much money there was. Father would catch my impatient glances, as I didn't dare ask anything aloud. A spark of our conversation would appear in his eyes. We understood each other. Father's eyes would tell me: "I love your mother. She is a good wife, and a good companion. Your mother doesn't waste the money, she handles it well, and makes excellent meals." Father enjoyed seeing our mother happy, and she appreciated his care.

Those moments when he was in *ćejf* and called her Gagula, and when she was counting money were brief. My mother's daily chores and her care for her children weighed heavily on her. The very next morning after happily counting the money my father had brought home, she would forget how happy she had been the night before, and how she had enjoyed counting the money. She would also forget that her family needed her love.

After a few evenings my father would have enough of talking about the misfortunes of his family and stories about the dead. Days, months, even years would go by where my father would not ask me to record anything. And then suddenly, his desire to record "lest it be forgotten" would rekindle within him. This never occurred when he was sober, only after he had his carafe of brandy and a shot glass. Mother would unwillingly set it for him on a platter, together with some *meze* to eat. With her eyes, she would let him know how much she disliked these drinking and writing sessions. As if not noticing her anger, father would toast to himself in a quest to find the beginning of his story. I didn't know anymore which was the beginning and which was the end of the story, or even whether or not it would be possible to understand what I was writing.

*   *   *

My father wanted me to record stories about women in his family who he loved and had tried to help in the past.

"Before she married my father, Alija Tahirović, my mother was first married to someone in Goražde. From that first marriage, she had a daughter called Rabija. I don't know if she fled from her first husband or if she divorced him, but I grew up with my half sister Rabija and I always loved her. She was very much like my mother, courageous and diligent, and she looked after all of us."

My father never pronounced anyone's name with as much love and respect as he did his sister Rabija's. This was probably because she reminded him so much of his mother, and of the beautiful childhood memories that he had of these women. They looked very much alike in photographs; tall and slender, with their long braided hair covered by kerchiefs, dark pensive eyes, prominent cheekbones, full and wide lips, and a somewhat dark complexion. My grandmother my aunt were truly beautiful women in their youths. However, aunt Rabija suffered the same tragic fate as other Romani women in Gorica, by marrying a bully by the name of H—.

She tried to hide her suffering and the regular beatings at the hands of her husband as much as she could. The stress of it eventually left her with a goiter. She rarely sought protection from my father, despite knowing well that he would protect her. Perhaps this was because the only way my father could help was by the use of his fists. When my father would see his sister covered in bruises, he would go after her husband H— to show him how a man fights with a man.

My aunt would occasionally stay at our home, devastated from the beatings, and in state of fear. She never came alone, and was always accompanied by her children: Bahra, Nusreta, Fajko, Zajko, Čučo, Majda, Sija and Hajrudin-Međed. Naturally, she couldn't leave them behind.

She would stay with us, waiting for her husband H— to sober up and come to his senses. My father would threaten him, demanding that he promise to never beat his wife again, and to be a good father to his children. Once sober, H— would be willing to to make all these promises, but soon he would get drunk again and start abusing his family once more.

My aunt suffered in silence, as she didn't want to distress her brother. This cycle would keep repeating itself, and nobody could help my aunt break out of that vicious circle of violence. My father's threats to H— didn't help much, yet threatening the man was his only reasonable option when H— was drunk and violent towards his wife.

*   *   *

My father always tried to help women from his and my mother's family. And truth be told, my mother's relatives were not lucky with their marriages either. Especially unfortunate was mother's older sister Zdenka, who grew up with her, wearing the black rubber boots and suffering through their father cutting their hair with a knife.

She got acquainted with a fellow from Serbia, who came to Sarajevo as a soldier. Girls tend to believe all the romantic fairy-tales that men tell them... she certainly did.

Zdenka followed him, pregnant with his child, to his village near Kruševac in Serbia. After her arrival, she soon discovered that he already had a wife and a child. She decided to stay in the village— where else could she go with a child in her belly? Her father, Andrija, would never take her in. No one in her family knew where she was. After her first child, another one followed. Then, after giving birth to two children, she no longer stand either the foreignness of that world, nor the proximity of the man who promised to marry her but instead brought her only suffering.

I don't know how she made contact with my mother, but when my father heard how heartbroken she was, alone in that village, he drove to Kruševac to fetch her right away. She left her older son with his father, and brought to Sarajevo only her younger son, Goran, who was still a toddler.

But where could she have gone? No one from her family could have taken her in, even if they wanted to. My parents found a solution. They allowed her to stay in the basement of our house where uncle Ejub-Mehmed, whom we called Stari, also lived. My mother helped Zdenka financially until she found a job, working as a cleaning lady in a government building. She stayed with us for a long time. Like many other women among our relatives, she enjoyed my father's protection, and so did her son Goran.

Later, when she married Nusret Ibrišević, who worked as a messenger in the Government building, she had a daughter with him

called Sanja. She would come to visit us often thereafter, befriending
my mother anew, and ever grateful to my father for having rescued
her from Kruševac, and for giving her a roof over head thereafter.

Yet, when something upset her, she would become fiery and say
horrible things. As a child, I couldn't understand this. I always
wondered how grown-ups can have such mood-swings. One minute
they're loving towards one other, kissing hello, and wishing each other
well; then, a moment later, they argue and take offense, acting like
bitter enemies until their furry subsides.

*   *   *

There were other women in the family that caused my father grief like
Safija and Nura, his paternal half-sisters.

"My father had also been married to another woman before meeting my mother. With his first wife, Fatima, he had two daughters:
Nura and Safija. Nura married Arif Ferhatović, and there were no
children out of that marriage. Nura raised and cared for Arif's children from his previous marriage. My sister Safija shared a similar fate.
She married a Šiptar Rom called Fahrudin Selimović. They never had
children any children together either.

"But let us not forget my half brother Mušan Sejdić. His last name
is different than ours, as my *babo* Alija had him with a woman that
he couldn't marry. She married a man whose family name was Sejdić
from Zenica, and took Mušan along. The man gave Mušan his family
name. I like him also, and we look after and visit one another as if we
had grown up together. He married a fine woman called Mulija, with
whom he fathered five children.

"God didn't give Safija any children, but she looked after her step-
children. Fahrudin was a good man, but after his death there was no
longer place for my sister in his family's house in Zemun. Friends told
me that she suffered a great deal over there, and that even her children
mistreat her. So I went to Zemun and brought her here to stay with
us."

I also remembered aunt Safija, along with the many problems she
caused. She didn't live with us. My father had found her a place in
the house where his sister Mubera had once lived. Aunt Safija had a
narrow, white face with sunken, dark eyes, a reflection of the sorrow

and suffering endured among her husband's family in Zemun, and her illness, asthma.

Remembering the sad lives of his sisters made my father's eyes well up, and occasionally his tears would fall onto his glass of brandy. My aunt Safija brought upon my father much stress and shame. Once she settled into her room in Gorica, she started having coffee and socializing with other women. My father didn't approve of this, but he couldn't forbid it either. "She doesn't have a strong mind of her own. They will lead her onto bad paths," was the fear he frequently shared with us.

My father knew women well. He knew how his sister had lived in Zemun. It didn't take long for my aunt, for whom father provided room and board, to start begging in the streets of Sarajevo. We knew she was doing this, but tried to hide it from our father. But one day, while driving his taxi, he came upon her begging on the street all the same.

"I was shocked to see her doing that. She shames me! She shames our family! I give her plenty of money, she has an allowance from me, I buy groceries for her like I buy them for all of us. What is she doing, why does she humiliate me like this? Why is she listening to my enemies?"

My father was ashamed; his pride was hurt. Nobody in his family ever begged for money. Everyone lived off the tools of their trade as best as they could, such was the way of Sarajevan Roma. My father told his sister that nobody in the family had ever begged for money. He reminded her how their father had been a blacksmith, and how proud he was of his work. I guess this conversation made my aunt feel ashamed, and she promised that she would never beg again. She confided to my father who had put her up to it. It was our first neighbor, with whom my father had some unsettled business from his youth. He knew very well how fiercely my father had fought against his kin resorting to begging, and so he took his revenge through father's half sister Safija, who was a weak and pliable woman.

Aside from this incident, my father had few conflicts with our neighbors or his relatives. He despised gambling, cheating, and begging. He lent money to others without charging interest, and without taking assurance in gold jewelry, something that could be found even in the poorest Romani families. Often when he lent money, he would outright say that there was no need to return it.

"My son, it's not good to lend money; it creates enemies. The moment the debtor realizes that he has to pay back money he doesn't have, he becomes your enemy. That's why whenever I lend money, I immediately absolve the person. They'll repay it all the same if they can. And never sell anything to relatives—you will always be held accountable if something goes wrong."

My father forgave his half-sister Safija for the shame she brought upon him. She told him that she was charmed by those people, but that she was seeing things clearly once more. Then, soon after, she fell asleep, never to wake up again. My mother was the one who found her dead body in her room. Her asthma had suffocated her. She was buried according to Muslim custom.

Our aunt Nura, on the other hand, was never a source of problems for my father. Having no children of her own, she instead looked after step-children, and even us sometimes. She always came in a clean *kat* and her head covered with *šamija*. Her *dimije* always looked nice on her slender body. She was a beautiful woman, with fair complexion, green eyes similar to my father's, and rosy cheeks.

She loved us and our mother. She always set money aside to buy us presents. I still remember a beautiful fabric for a dress, which she had given to my mother as a present. When she would hug me, I always had the feeling that she wished I was her child.

In our Gorica, one would encounter much misery but much love also. Unconditional love, asking for nothing in return. Nura was proud of her brother Derviš, and she praised him a great deal. Her only vice was tobacco.

One night, months after aunt Safija died, my father jumped out of his sleep and said outloud: "Who is smoking here? The house is full of tobacco smoke." But no one was smoking. It was the middle of the night, and we were all asleep until he roused us. We wondered what was troubling him.

He got out of bed, and walked down the stairs to the lower floor where our kitchen was located. He wanted to make sure nobody entered the house. Then, as soon as he had reached the main floor, we heard banging at the front door.

My father opened the door, and on the doorstep, there stood aunt Nura's step-son. He was in tears: "Dedo, Nura died! Derviš, Nura

From left to right: Aunt Safija, cousin Sada, aunt Zineta, cousin Sabina, uncle Hamdo, cousin Hamo lying down, aunt Nura, uncle Stari (Mehmed), uncle Ramo, Dina, and cousin Zikrija.

passed away just minutes ago!"

My father sat down, in a state of shock, and the beginning of a quickly smothered wail rose from his throat. By the time he started getting dressed, mother was ready to go. She was always helping when someone died. She participated in all the religious customs, she bowed and prayed with others. After the two of them left for aunt Nura's house, I wondered how my father sense her death? Who gave him the sign, that sixth sense with which he smelled aunt's last cigarette.

The house was in mourning again. At times, I had the feeling that our sorrow for our departed never really left the house.

*   *   *

"Sit down, my son Dinda, and write."

As a child, I enjoyed sitting next to my father to record his dictations. But I did not understand why my father's motto, "lest it is forgotten", was so important to him. He worked constantly to try to improve our lives, but he felt it was still important to remember all that had passed. Our house was perhaps the most concrete example of this sentiment of his...

The Tahirović home was constantly being upgraded, yet it was also very old and had witnessed a great deal. Our family had lived in the same house for three generations by my grandfather's time. In those days, the house had only a single room. Running water and lavatories were located outside the house in the backyard. How difficult it was to go outside to the unheated wooden stall in the winter. Once my cousins married, instead of moving away from our grandfather's home, they built their own houses next to the old shack, creating a cluster of houses.

Ramo, my father's eldest brother, had five children. He worked in the furniture factory in Stup. When he was sober, he was a good and diligent man; but he drank a lot, and when drunk, he was a very different man. Many dreadful things took place in his house, as in many other poor Romani households impacted by alcoholism.

Ramo was often sent to rehab at Jagomir hospital, but that didn't help him much, because as soon as he was released, he would start drinking again. And as soon as he was drunk once more, he would become aggressive towards his wife and children anew. When his children grew up, they reciprocated evil with evil. His daughters had lost all respect for him, and my father would often have to visit their house during the night to diffuse their conflicts. Evil from one family spread onto other families, the saying goes.

Ejub-Mehmed, the second eldest, worked for the printing house of the daily newspaper "Oslobođenje". His wife, auntie Anđa, worked as a cook in the "Ljubica Ivezić" home for orphans. Anđa wasn't Roma, she was Serbian from the distant village of Petrinja, close to Bosanska Kostajnica. I don't know how she came to marry our uncle, but she was part of the family. We all lived close to one another, and we all knew what was happening with each other. Mehmed and Anđa always treated us as if we were their children, as they had none of their own. My uncle was a man of few words, but he always invented stories for us. He even told us one day that he made each of us with his hammer and anvil in his blacksmith's workshop, and that's why we were all such beautiful children.

Auntie Anđa was always around when our mother needed to go to town on some errand. I have mostly happy memories of her, but also some painful ones, which I will tell you about later.

Our father also decided to improve our house by adding a second storey with a second room and a small kitchen. Under the staircase leading upstairs, there was enough room for an eventual bathroom. Then a few more years later, he added yet one more storey and another room.

From the upper bedroom, there was an exit onto the balcony; and from the balcony, a metal staircase led to the top of the house. Eventually, our father used concrete to create a permanent flat roof for the house. We often sat on top of that roof, and often had dinner in the open air.

Back when our house had only a single storey, we all used to sleep together in one room, mother, father, and children. Our parents slept on the couch, while we slept on mattresses spread out onto the floor; with the exception of my youngest sister, who slept next to mother because she was still being breastfed.

We were overjoyed when our father had built up to add that room on the second floor. I was about nine years old at that time. On the upper floor, there were two beds for the four of us, so we two of us slept on each bed. When one of us didn't feel like sharing anymore, she would take a mattress, or a thicker foam and would make a bed from it on the ground. I got along well with my sisters for the most part. We did quarrel occasionally, mostly over dresses we borrowed from one another without asking; but it was all quite innocent.

The entire village was our backyard. Our street was divided into many small streets going downhill, so that houses appeared as if they were sprouting out from the valleys. It seemed like everyone in the village was upgrading their homes. As elders were passing away, youngsters began to add rooms for their young families. Some people were moving out into city apartments, selling their houses to Šiptar Roma from Kosovo.

Most families had four, five, or more children. In our family, there were the four of us sister from my mother Dragica, our half-sister Jasminka from my father's first marriage, and eventually our brother, years later by the time the rest of us had mostly grown up.

My father would advise everyone who asked or was willing to listen on how to live a better life, and he was saddened by the fact that many of his relatives were dying from alcohol. But even in our home, there was not much goodness; our father and our mother fought constantly.

Our mother was nervous and angry whenever father came home in a state of ćejf. His stories bothered her; especially his "lest it is forgotten". As I sat next to him, ready to record, she would walk around us, glaring at me conspicuously, as though it was my fault that he would continue his drinking.

I enjoyed our special times together, feeling like he was the best father in the world that I could have ever had. I didn't want mother's anger to ruin our moment, though I knew she had the right to be angry with him.

*   *   *

When I was a very young child, the year prior to my starting school, there was a poor Romani family who was staying in our basement, having had no place else to go. They had several children, one of whom was M—, a tall, slender girl, who always wore a *dimije*. She was always home, helping my mother with housework, and taking care of us children. M—'s mother, A—, was known to have strange powers. Women who wished their rivals harm, or girls who wanted to marry a man who didn't love them would come to her. A—'s nick-name was "black magic woman", and her black magic was stronger than regular people's willpower.

I don't know how she worked her magic, but my mother felt the strength of A—'s powers. It appeared to us that A— wanted to hurt my mother, so that with her passing, M— could marry my father. And sure enough, Mother fell very ill and was unwell for most of their stay. One evening, as she was passing by the house, she saw a burning tree. Frightened, she kicked at the illusion, wanting to keep the fire away from the house, but suddenly fainted.

M— brought her into the house, gave her water, and took care of her; but my mother lost her trust towards both M— and her family that day. She was certain that A— was using black magic to try to destroy her marriage. Soon thereafter, the family was asked to leave our house.

Perhaps it was not soon enough though. M—'s spirit remained with us forever, as my father never forgot about her. Nobody knew whether it was mere fascination or the black magic, but she tied herself to him with her youth and beauty. He was a married man, who never promised to marry her; but women used to say that M— might even preferred it that way. After all, she didn't have to wash and cook for him, or deal with him when he was drunk. Father took care of her, and she never lived in poverty again.

My mother's intuition always told her when father was visiting the other woman. We all suffered after she entered into our world, and refused to leave his. In the beginning, my father denied everything; but the truth could never remain hidden in Gorica.

Their arguments would begin as soon as my father entered our home; it was as though this woman was still living with us. As my parents were fighting, they would constantly yell her name: "M—" or "M— A—". That's how we first found out about her and my father.

I always wished they would just hide things like this from us. The world of grown-ups was complicated and sometimes seemed beyond comprehension. One horrible word that was too often heard in our house was "abortion". My mother used to go to see a woman who did it secretly in her house, away from prying eyes. Who knows what sort of place it was... but obviously the woman could not have been a professional.

One time, I overheard a conversation between my mother and her sister Zdenka. They kept repeating the same word over and over again: abortion, abortion. It turned out that my mother and aunt Zdenka were taking M— to see that woman. M— had begged them for help, because she found herself pregnant from our father. But neither of them wanted to have a child together, and even M— didn't want him to leave his family to go to live with her; so they decided that she should have an abortion.

It so happened that my mother was pregnant too. Indeed, I can hardly remember her without a pregnant belly; and the regular burden of her pregnancies was steadily ruining her nerves. And we, her children, could tell. Whenever our mother was overly nervous, or whenever she beat or punished us without good reason, we knew that she had to be with child.

And now she was confronted by the shame of that woman, with a belly to match her own, who claimed that she didn't want to take my father away from her and his children. Back then, I didn't understand these things too well; but I remember that the atmosphere in our home was unbearable.

Mother just kept crying and complaining to her sister, "What am I going to do, Zdenka? I cannot handle any more shame. I cannot hurt my children by having this woman carry this adulterous child. If she wants to abort this pregnancy, we'll take her to that woman."

When it was finally over and my mother had returned, she walked around the house as if carrying a burden of sadness on her shoulders. She had a headache that would not pass, and was venting her pain and sorrow on us children. She was also quarreling constantly with our father, who just kept repeating that he loved us and would never leave us.

*   *   *

Something else I found bewildering was how as soon as somebody mentioned father's sister Rabija, he would immediately start cursing her husband H—. Whenever he had a few drinks, he'd shout to nobody in particular, "One day I'll show him, for all those beatings!' Rabija is constantly bruised from his hands." Then he would start choking from his tears, and rush out into the street, telling us, "I'm going to visit my sister, to make sure he didn't hurt her today!"

My father was pained by his sister's sadness of the daily abuse she had to face. He wanted so much to help her, to make her husband come to his senses and stop beating her. But there was only so much he could do.

Growing up, several unanswered questions formed in my mind. Whenever my father would defend his sister, I would crouch in a corner, wondering if one day my life would be like aunt Rabija's. And would my father be powerful enough to protect me from the man that I would marry? What's more, would he be able to protect all five of his daughters?

And who was defending my mother? Why wasn't there anybody coming to our home to defend her when father is beating her? Was my father's soul also pained by our mother's suffering? Was he pained also when he punishes us for one or another simple childish mischief?

Though his punishments all had innocent names, they were all quite severe. If we made a mistake, however small, we got a so called "father's lesson", which was having to stand in place for hours in front of our father. For bigger mistakes, we were punished by "flips" of his hand, but the "flips" were actually slaps on the face. Nobody ever came to rescue us from those punishments...

During his "father's lessons" he would sometimes spend hours telling stories about well-behaved children, and what would happen if we failed to be obedient. He never tired of talking, but our legs all the more quickly grew numb for the strain of standing so still for so long. Me and my sisters called his "father's lessons", "father's torture". We would stand still, lined up in front of father, like soldiers facing a general. If one of us made the slightest movement, his "lesson" would last longer and the pain in our legs would have more time to grow stronger still.

If we frowned, or if he caught even just a hint of disagreement or defiance in our eyes, the punishment would continue with us being sent into the corner to kneel on dry corn kernels. They would stick to our knees and our legs leaving deep marks from our own weight upon them. The pain of this was so intense that tears would well in our eyes. Our souls were hurting too, because we didn't believe that these punishments were fair, we didn't believe they were coming from the same father that we loved so much. He protected us from outsiders, but no one could protect us from his punishments, which only got worse with time.

When he thought we made a bigger mistake, he would slap each of us in the face, one after the other, as if by some sort of chain reaction. For him though, these were not real slaps, that's why he jokingly called them "flips". We would line up, from eldest to youngest, and he would slap us, one after the other. Whenever he did this, I would picture in my mind images of car crashes, just like they always showed on television. If we protested, that only meant more of father's "flips".

Nobody ever came to our defense during those times, not even our own mother. I could never understand her. She would come over to recount to him our disobedience, adding fuel to the fire, making our punishments increase. We would get yet another round of "flips"; this time in reverse order, from youngest to eldest. His hand always felt heavy on our small cheeks. Afterwards, our heads hurt and we would wear his fingerprints on our faces for days.

Other times, it was our mother's turn, and her head would hurt even more than ours did, because father always hit her harder than he hit us. She was his wife, a woman whom he would never leave for another; yet, he constantly beat her because of the other woman in his life. She would never quietly accept the fact that he was cheating on her.

They were horrible nights; nightmares I would rather forget. I and my sisters would hide in corners, crouched with our heads between our knees, blocking our ears with our hands to stop ourselves from hearing mother's screams, bending our heads down to stop ourselves from seeing what was happening at the other end of the room. Even as father would hit mother, she would carry on quarreling and shouting, and there was nowhere to hide from her screams.

It seemed very clear in those moments that mother's punishment was far worse than our own punishments ever got. My sisters and I just cried in our corner throughout it all, but we never dared to come to her help, as we were afraid of him too. Except once...

One evening, my sister Alma, the bravest of us all, couldn't take it anymore when father started hitting mother. Alma lost all her fears in an instant, grabbed onto a chair, got on her tip-toes to try to rise to our father's height even as he was getting ready to take another swing at mother. Then she hit him with chair. Then swung the chair and hit him a second time.

I admired her courage. Surprised, our father stopped for a moment, staring into the eye of his a child with the chair in her hands. Though she hadn't hit him that hard, and he certainly wasn't hurt, he stood bewildered and perplexed by her courage. He didn't hit mother again that night.

We were petrified to see what would happen next. Our father sat down, holding his face in those palms, whose powers we all remembered so vividly, and he told Alma: "My child raised her hands on me! My daughter, you are the same as your nana, my courageous mother Mejra, who feared nothing."

There was one particular story about courageous nana Mejra that we heard countless times. I even recorded it once during father's dictations:

Mother held all four corners of the house, as the saying goes, because my father Alija spent much of his time in his blacksmith's workshop on Koševo's Hill. One evening after dinner, as everyone was getting ready to go to bed, we heard footsteps outside the house. I was feeling afraid , but not my mother Mejra. She took removed some ember from the oven fire and marched outside, ready to defend her home and her family. When implored by her children to stay, she simply motioned that the unwanted guest was going get hot ember in the eyes, if he dared to approach the house.

Now father was watching his daughter Alma, who displayed courage in defending her mother from his tyranny. Two courageous women, one with glowing ember, the other with a chair in her hands. It seemed like my father was ashamed of himself. For the first time ever, he just sat there without ever mentioning punishment such disobedience would normally have garnered. From that evening onward, father never again beat our mother, and he also stopped giving out his "flips". Even the word "flip" turned into a joke thereafter. He would sometimes jokingly ask: "Why aren't you listening, do you want a 'flip'?" At first, the question would raise our alarm; but as the threat was never again followed-through, our fear eventually dissipated, and father's "flips" remain a source of humour among us even to this day.

*   *   *

Father realized that Alma was now a grown woman, and permitted her after the incident with the chair to dress the way she wanted. He even let her wear *dimije*, though he didn't approve of it. He also didn't like long hair on young girls, and considered it, along with *dimijes*, to be symbols of our Gorica's primitivism; forms of untimely pressure on our girls to grow up ahead of time. "They look like women, but their hair is still filled with nit and lice. Why are they in such a hurry to grow up? Let them be children!"

He understood the problems Romani girls faced. He knew how difficult it was to escape the tradition of early marriage, and the life-time of troubles they could bring. It was for this reason that he always wanted to control and protect us, the reason he wanted to prevent us from growing up. It was a habit that stayed with him even into our adulthood. And though the "flips" may have stopped, father instituted other rigorous measures meant to educate us.

He would get terribly angry whenever we violated his rules. He was always very clear about which children from our village we were allowed to play with, and which ones we were to avoid. Father knew the kind of parents our neighbors were, and never allowed us to play with children whose parents didn't care about cleanliness or education.

I actually agreed with this rules of his. After playing with dirty, uncombed children, we would get lice in our hair. Lice were always a real problem in Gorica. I still remember vividly how itchy our scalp would become, and how we would scratch without pause.

Father was also afraid that he might catch lice from us during, knowing that it would have been very detrimental for him as a taxi driver. "What would I do? Imagine the shame of my colleagues and my customers spotting lice on my head. They would not let me get anywhere near the taxi stop anymore!"

Our mother would always beat us when we got lice. It was easy to get them, but it took days to get rid of them. Mother had to comb five heads using a thick comb with braided cotton. She would take a large white sheet of paper, bend our heads over it and pushed the thick comb as hard as she could, getting the comb's teeth to scrape against our skulls in order to get both the lice and the nits. It hurt dreadfully, and as she was combing our head, lice would fall onto the paper like grains of rice. How repugnant that sight was on the white paper. This ritual would last for hours, sometimes repeated for several days in a row. Wearing short hair was thus good advice from our father. It made getting rid of the lice faster—but it was no prevention, and we kept getting them again and again from various neighbors' children.

Even when our father was rigorous or downright unjust, even when he was punishing us for insignificant mischief by raising his heavy hand on us, he never forgot that he was our father and never once withdrew his care and protection for us. There was always an abundance of food in the house, and he always tried to advise us as best as he could.

*   *   *

It was always a special occasion for us when father bought food from the grocery carriages that local peasants would regularly bring to Gorica. While many community services, the trash collectors among them, would frequently pass us by without stopping; Abid and Alijaga, the owners of the grocery carriages, would come to us as happily as if they were returning home.

They even seemed to be motivated to do good deeds, and would permit those would couldn't pay to buy on credit. Many a child's belly was full during the week only because those two didn't see us as "cigani". They never called us pejorative names and never gave us dirty looks, like so many others. And they never refused our coffee, when it was offered to them. They even joked with us, and occasionally offered kids free fruit from their bushels.

And we children weren't even most excited about the food, but rather the horses! It was thrilling to see such large animals strolling down our streets. This is one of my fondest memories from Gorica. I admired the strength of those horses, the beautiful shape of their bodies, and those big eyes that would look at us with so much wisdom.

Alijaga and Abid would hold the horses so we could pet them, knowing how excited we were during these visits. What a pleasure it was to pet a horse's neck next to its mane. As a child, I would often draw horses, thinking about the mighty men in my family: my grandpa, my uncles, and my father, who were all skilled in horseshoeing. If I had been a boy, I would have probably learned the trade as well.

Whenever my father heard the sound of hooves during our dictations, he would jump to his feet and head toward the door. He knew the carriage would stop in front of our house, because the peasants knew that they would be able to make good bargains with my father, and that he would pay upfront for everything he bought.

Abid would be the first to appear at the door, selling milk, cheese, fruit jams, and vegetables. As our house had many children, and often several more guests, we needed plenty of food. My father would sometimes buy up all the food pulled by Abid's horse. And as soon as Abid got paid, Alijaga would show up in his place, bringing fresh fruits and vegetables from his garden and lovely wool socks knitted by his wife, which father used to buy us for winter.

Alijaga's garden was right next to our *mahala*. He and his wife worked diligently to grow the fruits and vegetables he sold. They were Bosnian Muslims, who never shied away from visiting us, and would sometimes come by in the evening just to sit and talk.

Most of produce that Abid and Alijaga brought could be conserved for winter months, when deliveries were scarce. But father usually waited for one more salesman, "When Petko arrives, we'll buy from him smoked meat and home-made plum brandy. His plumb brandy is the best!"

Once all the peasants left our house, father would remember that he wanted to record yet another story about his family. But which one? He would pick up his brandy and food again, and I waited in vain for the story to commence, while daydreaming about those beautiful horses.

Thanks to Abid's and Alijaga's generosity many children in our *mahala*, who might otherwise have gone hungry, were able to eat. We Tahirović sisters instinctively understood how different our father was, and how hard he worked to ensure that our needs and wants were met. From an early age, as we learned about the world around us, our love for our father grew ever greater from a mixture of fear and respect. The love we felt for our father and the awe he inspired, stayed with us until the day he died. Even today we remember him with immense love and respect... he never hesitated to take care of those who needed his protection.

*   *   *

When we were children, he was more concerned about our health than that of our mother. If one of us would cough even just once, he would immediately jump to his feet to try to determine the nature of our illness. Mother would try to convince him that "it was nothing", but he wouldn't accept her assessment and wanted to see for himself whether we were healthy. He would take us onto his lap, and would feel our forehead for fever and ask if we were in any pain.

There were times when his worry wasn't all that pleasant. He had his own remedies for every ailment, and as soon as he would notice the first sign of a cold, he would start preparing one of his remedies to stop the cold from becoming worse. But this remedy usually consisted of a plate of chopped garlic, covered with oil and vinegar, sprinkled with salt and pepper, all mixed with a bit of water. He would serve this remedy with bread, urging us to dip our piece into the mixture and eat it alongside our regular food.

If after ingesting his remedy, we still had high fever, he would take the next step. He would grate an unpeeled potato to mix with vinegar and water. Then he would take two linen cloths, and after soaking them in cold water, he would fill them with his potato and vinegar mixture, and proceed to wrap the cloths around our feet. This was father's way of lowering our fever.

Father believed that people were envious of him because of his lovely children. He also superstitiously believed that we were sometimes affected the evil eyes of our neighbors and relatives. When my younger sisters cried during the night, he would recite a sura from the Qur'an, as a ritual to break whatever spells were upon his children. As part of the rirtual, he would touch his child's forehead with his tongue, and then spit towards the four corners of the room, saying "Shoo, shoo! Go away, you Devil!" Other times, when we happened to fall while running about, He used his spit as a balm upon the cuts on our arms or legs. And, indeed, our wounds always healed quickly.

His special remedies could heal anything, and we were rarely sick, and when we were, we always recovered quickly. This was part of father's care for my sisters and I, and it served always to strengthen our relationships with him.

Unfortunately, no such bond existed with our mother. Our relationship with her had always bothered me since my childhood. We needed a strong mother, like our grandmother Mejra. We needed a woman who could handle and confront life's problems when they arose. But our mother Dragica instead wanted to forget it all: her childhood, her cruel father, her prior life in poverty. At least she didn't forget her own mother, our grandma Ankica, despite her having left mother as a child with her alcoholic father. In fact when Grandma came to visit us, love seemed to fill our whole house.

The problem was that my mother had forgotten why she had married our father; she never wanted to talk about it. She suffered because of other women in her life, especially because of M—. She mentally escaped to some imaginary world of her own, as a way to avoid all her motherly responsibilities. In many respects, the life of the poorer Roma in Gorica was a lot more familiar to her than it had ever been to us.

She would not let us stay in bed in the mornings, not even if we were sick. Having us in the house in the morning bothered her, as that was her time of freedom, to do the things father despised most. She would use this time to visit neighbors or to receive them in our home. This was her time for having coffee and fortunetelling. From the Romani women, mother learned fortunetelling from the coffee grounds and also the Romani language. Soon she surpassed them, when it came to fortunetelling. She read entire stories from the leftover grounds, and the other women would always claim that she had got it right.

As if it was difficult to predict what was going to happen in Gorica. Mother knew what trouble was all about, as men always came home drunk to beat their wives, and always eventually left for another woman. It was easy to determine a person's upcoming misfortunes just by looking into their eyes.

Despite mother's ability to divine other people's troubles, she was often cruel to us. It was as though she was learning all the wrong lessons from some of the other Romani women, who not only were unable to show proper love to their children, but would take their frustrations out on their children whenever someone was cruel to them.

On mornings when mother would try to kick us out of bed even though we were sick, our father would try to protect us, telling her "What is it Dragica? Leave the child be, she's got fever and she is sick! Good God, this woman must have a heart of stone, she is so cold..."

She would beat us for the smallest mischief when he wasn't around. But it was easier to take than her swearing. Father forbade the use swearing and bad words, and she would avoid them also when he was home. But once he wasn't around, she would swear and call us all kinds of names. I was most often her main target, on account of being so much like my father.

It is true that we had our mother's white skin, but what we didn't have was her love. She was so much like our worst neighbors; aggressive, bad tempered women. Not at all like some of the other Romani women, who raised their children with love and care even in the face of a harsher and more difficult life than my mother had to put up with.

When mother got upset with our father, it was only a matter of time before she would direct her anger and frustration towards us. We didn't understand why it was that way, but we suffered in silence. And with her, silence was golden. Any attempt to protest only brought on more beatings, and her reporting our behavior to our father, who would top it all off with a lecture.

In those days, a great state of fear began to grow inside of me, from all the things happening around us. Mother not only didn't feel that fear, but herself created ever more of them for me. I was mostly afraid of her state of nervousness when she was pregnant, though I pitied her too, knowing that she was aching all over. But despite my sympathy, I just felt like I needed someone to protect me from my fears... and she only amplified them.

*   *   *

Back in those days when we didn't yet have a bathroom or a bathtub, my mother washed us in a cauldron in the kitchen. We children were responsible for bringing water into the house from the street fountain, and she, in turn, would warm the water in the kettle on the stove.

One evening, Mother was especially nervous. She was rough and inattentive as she bathed us, failing to ensure that the water had cooled enough or that the soap didn't get into our eyes. When my turn came, I was afraid of being bathed. Mother placed me into the tin cauldron and rubbed me with soap until my head was covered with foam.

She was rubbing washing and shampooing me so hard it hurt, and she didn't pay attention when she decided to rinse me down. She hastily submerged a one liter jug in the water in the kettle, and poured the water over my head. Her sudden motion startled me, and I didn't have time to close my mouth, so the soap from my hair got into my mouth, and I started choking even as more soap came down and into my mouth, still open amidst my choking. She didn't notice what had happened and kept pouring more water. Somehow I managed to catch my breath, and started to scream. Mother didn't understand why I was screaming, so she continued on pouring more water over me, while hitting me all over and screaming hysterically to get me to shut up.

I'll never forget that traumatic experience. I have been petrified of hair-washing or even just being in water ever since. It also lead to my suffering from panic attacks whenever I would pull clothes down over my head while getting dressed... the sensations just immediately recalled the terror of that evening.

If it had been anyone else that had done that to me, I would surely have hated them for it. But I never hated my mother. I only longed for her love, and, in its absence, missed her my entire life. Yet I could never talk about this, not even in my adulthood.

In Gorica, there was no escape from such a life. Everybody lived that way. Our *mahala* was calm only when it rained and when it was cold. We Roma do not like the rain or the snow, or anything else that keeps us from the outdoors. And when outdoors, every family's troublesome life flooded straight out into the *mahala*. Husbands would beat their wives and children right in front of their neighbors. Everybody swore constantly, as if nobody knew any nice words. Fights among neighbours and women's quarrels were breaking out all the time. Occasionally even knifes would be brandished. Nobody could tell anymore who was enemy with whom or even for what reason... then just ust a few hours later, men would sit together drinking brandy and women would sip coffee together once more during their lengthy fortunetelling sessions. Even when they didn't predict trouble, misfortune was sure to come!

*   *   *

My father's favourite place was the Turbe, a hill-top clearing where one could still see the remnants of old overgrown Turkish tombs. There was a water reservoir surrounded by a wire fence in the Turbe. When we visited as a family, we would sit in the shade, close to the wire fence, next to a tall yellow flowering shrub. Father would always remind us to sit in the shade, "so that we don't get sunburnt worse yet, a sunstroke". Mother would often bring pots filled with already prepared food. The Turbe was our oasis.

Sometimes father went there by himself during his lunch-hour to try to catch a nap. He always sought to retreat to the Turbe in order to avoid the noise of our *mahala*. He was bothered by the quarrels and the constant loud music of the cassette-players. He often wanted to get some rest, and this was impossible to do in our *mahala*. He suffered the most when Roma newcomers would hold their weddings and sunets They would bring entire orchestras with elaborated sound systems for these occasions, and what sounded like very monotonous music just wouldn't stop for three days.

I also had no place to escape the music and concentrate on my studying. To me, my books were my escape from the *mahala*. I had my place at home in the corner, under the picture of my paternal grandfather, Alija Tahirović. But the sound of music would infiltrate even there. I would cover ears with my hands and read out loud, louder, even louder only to be able to concentrate on my reading.

Only at the Turbe, in the world of the deceased, could one find peace. I especially like going there with father, who often lay in the shade to sleep. But we only went there during the day, because it was said that ghosts visited it at night.

Grandfather Alija Derviš Tahirović

One of the more popular ghost stories about the Turbe was about a man returning home from work, who dared to walk through the Turbe at night. It is said that he encountered a goat in his path. The goat started to kick him, and even somehow managed to grab onto his throat. The animal was quite heavy, and the man had a hard time standing up. He took a few steps back, then stopped and then tried to walk again. But the goat wouldn't let go of his throat and was pressing it even more. The man didn't understand what was happening to him, and by then could barely stand on his feet. Only when the man suddenly staggered into a glimpse of the lights from the *mahala* did the goat jump away to disappear into the night.

It is said that the next day, when the man recounted what had happened, everybody agreed that a ghost from the Turbe acted in a revenge for his disturbing the dead at night. Indeed, the man supposedly didn't live longer after that, and fell sick and died shortly thereafter.

Was there any truth to this story? We didn't care, since we only went to the Turbe during the day to seek the peace that we eluded us in our *mahala*, and respected peace of the dead during the night.

*   *   *

In Gorica, it was customary to jokingly scare children by saying "Into the house, quickly, ghosts are coming!" They also used to scare us with some specific ghosts: Javišta, Karandžoloz and Karankoči-koči. And we children were very afraid of them, even though we had no idea who or what they were.

I could never understand why parents and neighbors of children from other Sarajevo *mahalas* would try to frighten them by saying "If you do bad things, or if you venture away from our house, *Cigani* will kidnap you and take you away from your home!" I watched my neighbors, many of whom were uneducated, quarrelsome, and frequently drunk, but not one of them had ever kidnapped another person's child.

I thought such ugly scare tactics were gravely unjust. Even incomprehensible, as the Roma, unlike most everyone else, did not treat others with instant prejudice, and never insulted anybody merely because of their religion or nationality. Not to mention that they certainly didn't need other people's children, as they had plenty of their own.

Despite the ugly warnings children elsewhere may have gotten, our own parents only ever frightened us with imaginary creatures, but never said things like, "If you go there, Muslim *balije* will steal you, or the Orthodox will take you away!"

The children from Gorica had a strong phobia about mice. While Gorica was close to the center of the city, the municipal services were very scarce. Sometimes the garbage wasn't removed for months at a time, and there were mounds of it lying everywhere. It was a paradise for mice, and they multiplied at a rapid pace, making their way into every single household. Our home was no exception. It was scary to think about mice running around our *mahala*, invading homes, and walking over our personal belongings; but we couldn't fight them the way we fought lice.

I remember one incident that happened when mother and father had gone to the city and left us home by ourselves. We were all sitting in the room on the ground floor, making sure that the fire didn't die out. We kept adding more and more wood onto the fire, knowing that while the fire burned, we would stay warm. Then suddenly a mouse ran out of our woodpile, and we all jumped up in horror to get away from it. I climbed onto the window, Jasminka onto the table, and Alma onto the bed and our screams echoed through the *mahala*.

The mouse ran to the middle of the room, stood on our blanket, and looked at us peacefully. Those small black eyes appeared so frightening to us. It kept watching us, taking the occasional walk around the blanket, then walked behind the stove and crawled under the blanket. Our brave Alma took that opportunity and jumped from the bed. She took a piece of wood and started pounding what she thought was the contour of the mouse's small body underneath the blanket. The mouse squeaked and was suddenly back out from underneath the blanket, jumping about chaotically. To us, it appeared like it was trying to jump onto us. Its eyes were big with fear, and suddenly Alma threw her piece of wood down and jumped back onto the bed. When we realized that even our brave sister had retreated, we screamed even louder.

Fortunately, having heard our screams, *amidža* Mehmed's wife Anđa had arrived. She always looked after us whenever our parents were away. She stood at the doorstep, searching for some dangerous intruder with her gaze. When she realized that our intruder was quite tiny and squeaking on the floor, she started laughing out loud even as the little mouse made its escape. "Just a mouse? For God's sake children, I thought someone had attacked you!" she chuckled, then took us to her home to make us feel safe until our parents returned.

*   *   *

Our father always found ways to make us happy, ways to fulfill our childhood wishes. When we asked him for a dog, he brought us a puppy that he got from a peasant. The puppy was quite large, but as he still drank milk, we used to feed him with milk from nursing bottles. One day, our uncle Fahrudin was visiting, and when he observed our puppy's curious way of sprawling out in his sleeping box, he jokingly remarked, "Look at the puppy, he's lying like a real *paša*!" And that's just what we decided to name him!

While Paša was still a puppy, he spent his time with us in the kitchen. He was growing fast, but we didn't know what breed he was, or whether he was even mixed. He looked like a German shepherd though, and when he grew too big to stay inside, father built him a dog house just outside our front door. Even after that, when it was cold or when it rained too much, we made room for our Paša in the front hall.

He may have been just a plain brown dog like so many others in Sarajevo, but to us, Paša was the best and the smartest dog. He would play with us, and follow us to school, not permitting anyone to get near us. We loved him, and he loved us! He would even wait for us after school and went with us to the market in Marijin Dvor or where else we'd have to go. He would accompany me when I went to visit grandma Ankica in Pofalići or to the Turbe; he often guarded father's car, and would run after him when he left to work. His hearing was so acute that he would hear our father's car even before he entered our *mahala*, and he would run out all the way to the Turbe to wait for him.

We never got as much love from most people as we did from our Paša. But it was also rare for a dog to get as much love from its owners as Paša did. We never beat him, and only gave him the finest food. The whole *mahala* knew him and loved him—he was a source of great pride for us.

Occasionally municipal services or somebody from the town would become concerned that mice from our *mahala* would infest the rest of the city, and they would send workers to put out rat poison. We never thought that these afterthought attempts at pest control would bring such tragedy upon our family.

One day, Paša ran into the house and up the stairs, trying to enter our room. We had never before seen him so distraught, as he was that day. He was in a state of panic, barking, and waiving his tail. He was trying to tell us something, as if begging for our protection. We took him down to the front hall, and as we got closer, his speed increased. In front of the house, he suddenly lay down on top of father's feet. Father immediately understood, and shouted to my mother, "Dragica, someone poisoned the dog! He must have eaten rat poison! Fetch some sour milk quickly!" But we didn't think the situation was so bad. We believed that our father would be able to save him. He tried pouring the sour milk into his mouth, begging him to swallow it. But the milk was only dripping down Paša's throat, as he didn't even have the energy to swallow anymore. He then started breathing heavily, and soon it was over.

We couldn't save him. Afterwards we felt that he probably knew that he couldn't be saved, and ran upstairs to get us because he wanted to die surrounded by those he loved. We cried and mourned for our Paša for a long time to come...

Occasionally our fear of mice and our grief for Paša would fade to give way to yet greater fears and sorrows. One such fear was that our mother would leave father and us, because of father's drinking and cheating. I never wanted that to happen, I didn't want another woman to replace my mother.

*   *   *

Not all of my memories form the Turbe are good. I remember there was a big fight between my parents one day. Father was fairly drunk, and mother reproached him angrily for coming home so late, crying and saying that she was miserable with him and would leave us all. We children crouched in the corner, petrified, and cried throughout their fight. We fell asleep only once their voices had calmed down.

Then, when father left for work in the morning, mother grabbed a few of her dresses, kissed us goodbye, and left the house. It wasn't the first time either. Whenever she couldn't handle the stress of her marriage anymore or felt neglected beyond her tolerance, she would leave with her belongings to go to her father, Andrija.

When our father came home during his breaks, he found us alone and hungry. He ushered us into his car and took us to the Turbe. Once there, he spread a blanket out onto the grass, and ordered us to sit down and start eating. He always brought a wide assortment of foods, including pies, hamburger meat, bread, tomatoes, and juice of some sort.

Even when our father was worried, he never neglected his responsibilities toward his children. He fed us one by one, placing bite sized portions of food into our mouths, as though he was feeding little chicks. In such moments, we would forget his "lessons" and his "flips", and with the glimmer of our eyes, we would tell each other that there can be no better father than ours in the whole wide world.

He kept silent for a long time, but eventually he asked us, "Do you want me to replace your mother with another woman?"

"No, we don't want another woman! We want only our mother!", we answered in unison and broke down into tears. We knew exactly who he had in mind, and we didn't want that other woman to take our mother's place.

Father would just shrug his shoulders, not wanting to go against our wishes. Then a few days later, he would drive to his father-in-law and bring our mother back home. Such was life for too many families, and I sometimes wondered whether women's miseries and men's drunkenness was perhaps hereditary.

My maternal grandmother Ankica was the only woman I knew who managed to escape the destiny of becoming a submissive wife. Born in 1919 in the Kingdom of Yugoslavia, she lived in a time when there were few schools for boys and none at all for girls from poor families like my grandmother. When she turned 14 years old, her family married her off to our grandfather, Andrija Vrebac, who was a butcher.

"I couldn't have been more unfortunate," she would tell me once I was old enough to understand what she meant. "Andrija was a man without a soul. He thought that I was his property, and that he could torture and humiliate me as he pleased!"

"I gave him two children, my daughter Matilda and my son Ivica. But it was the time before the war, and though we had nothing as it was, he would still spend all of his earnings in pubs and on women. Sarajevo winters being as they are, there icicles hanging from the walls even inside our home, and I had no wood at all with which to light a fire to warm up the room. Both my children died in my arms from the freezing cold.

"Then I gave birth to two more children, and in 1942, in the middle of the war, I gave birth to your mother Dragica. In those days, my husband would sometimes tie me up to a chair, and beat me for as long as he pleased. When the war was finally over, I couldn't take it anymore...

"I felt sorry for my children, but if I had not left my abusive husband, one of us would have killed the other soon enough, and my children would have been left without a mother either way. My uncle Antun was the only man willing to help me, and he let me live with him. He worked for the railway and had a single room at his disposal in Petra Mećave street, next to the old railway tracks. The room was fairly spacious so we partitioned it and we both had our own corner. He surely earned his way to Heaven for taking me in at a time when the rest of my family didn't want to hear about my troubles. In those days, women rarely left their husbands, not even those who were beaten and assaulted day after day.

"Once I had learned to read and write, I started looking for a job. I first became an assistant cook at the Municipal Hospital, and then a maid for a wealthy family. They even insured me and gave me a regular salary. Never again did I let anyone raise their hand at me. I learned to defend myself. Though it is true that my children never forgave me for leaving them behind; especially my youngest daughter, Mirjana."

Grandma Ankica gave me the warmth and love that my mother could not. She was a person that made my childhood sweeter and taught me many things about life. I could talk to her about anything, even the things that my parents never let themselves be bothered about.

Even though my grandma worked as a maid, she was always well dressed. She looked polished and refined. I can still see her, with her makeup and her lovely haircut. She would find great satisfaction in the little things in life.

Visiting her was always an experience. She always had the most delicious foods on her table, would sing popular songs and dance the Waltz. Her world was different from what I knew, and I wanted so much to live in that world. Even when she eventually married a younger Muslim man, who tried to discourage her from working, she refused, as she wanted to work and the independence of having her own money.

And she also needed money for us, her grandchildren. She was especially fond of me, her eldest granddaughter. When I would sleep over by her I would frequently wake up to find new shoes, books, and notebooks beside my bed. When she came to visit us in Gorica, she would bring sweets and always a can of fish for me, knowing how much I loved fish. She would also bring me various little things that girls would collect; in fact, thanks to her, I had the most beautiful napkins in all of our *mahala*. Whenever she came it was a special treat, not only because of the fish or the other presents, but simply because of the joy of knowing that my grandmother was thinking about me.

She and I enjoyed going for walks together. She was always in a good mood, and would laugh, joke around the whole time. She would also turn her head after good looking men, who, in turn, usually turned their own head to admire her, much to her delight. She wanted to remain beautiful and desirable, the way she couldn't in her youth because of her early marriage. She even told us grandchildren to call her auntie.

But I still called her grandma. I was proud to have such a beautiful and interesting grandmother. Her second husband did love us and treat us as his own grandchildren. Our father also loved his mother-in-law Ankica, but he didn't like the influence she had on us girls. She showed us too much freedom, and because of that, he only let us go visit her despite his better judgment. Though on the other hand, he always enjoyed dancing and drinking wine with her.

Grandma was always candid in her opinions about men. She often said that men shouldn't be taken seriously, because they don't think with their heads. She also believed that any woman who can find a man that she could drink coffee, talk, and joke with, probably found a man who understood her and was therefore truly fortunate.

Otherwise, men, in her view, never understood anything, and followed only their male instincts to chase after women; thinking all too rarely about their wives and children at home.

Had it not been for my grandmother's openness, her willingness to listen to my problems, and her attempts to show me all the beautiful things in the world, my childhood in Gorica would have been a lot more difficult and lonely. My grandma gave me warmth during the most difficult times. When there was trouble at home, she would say, "Let them be, you cannot change them. You have to be the patient one now. But when you grow up, don't let anyone use you or abuse you!"

*   *   *

Sometimes father wouldn't wait for me to write down his stories. He would take the notebook and the pencil and write his "lest it be forgotten" memories himself. Even when he didn't remember all the details, he at least wrote down the general things; recounting names of the living and deceased members of his family, and that of my mother's. And as much as he could, he tried to describe only the happier aspects of his own life.

Journal Entry by Derviš Tahirović, 1983.

It is customary for Roma to get married young. I myself was barely 19 when I married Mulija S—. I was with her for a year and we had a daughter, Jasminka. But she wasn't a good wife, she wasn't proper, so I asked her to leave, and when she did, little Jasminka stayed with me.

It was soon afterwards that I met my sweetheart at the Slaviša Vajner Čiča school. I had always wanted to marry a blonde woman like my Dragica. When she agreed to be my wife, I brought her to my house in Gorica and married her right away, because I saw that she was a decent woman, and I didn't want to live out of wedlock with her. We have been married for 24 years now, and in addition to Jasminka (my daughter from my previous wife), we have five more children: our daughters Hedina, Alma, Ehlimana, Elvira, and our son Alin.

I can say that we have a good relationship, and that we live well, taking into account that we come from different cultures. We never listened to other people's opinions, and didn't let anybody influence our marriage to ruin our pleasant marital life. Dragica respected my Romani roots, and never cursed my parents or my ancestry. Our mutual respect for each other was due to the love we felt for one another. Our life should be viewed as an example of love, respect, and friendship in a mixed marriage.

Dragica's parents were Catholics and didn't object to her marrying me. Dragica's mother Ankica Perušić was born on June 19th,1919. She is a good grandmother to our children. A woman who always loved and respected me as her son-in-law. Ankica's own parents were named Tomo and Lucija Perušić, and she three brothers, Ivo, Anto, and Drago, and one sister, Sofija. (Only Ankica and Ivo ever had children. Ankica has my wife Dragica, and also Zdenka and Mirjana. Ivo has three children from two different wives. With his first wife, he had Miroslav and Mirjana, and with his second wife he had Mario.)

Dragica's late father, Andrija Vrebac, was born on November 29th, 1912 to his father Marko and his mother Kate. He had a brother called Joseph and a sister called Ivanka-Ikica, who came to raise Andrija's daughter Mirjana. Ikica also had two sons, Slavko and Marko. Slavko Vrebac became a well-known soccer player with "Željezničar". He was very athletic, but he disappeared, no doubt died, quite young. Marko, on the other hand, is thankfully still alive and well.

In our family, we do not let culture or ethnicity become a basis for prejudice. Dragica's mother, Ankica, had married a Muslim man, called Mujanović Ramiz, later in her life. Dragica's sister Zdenka also married a Muslim man, called Nusret Ibrišević; and their other sister, Mirjana, had married Ivo Grlić, with whom she had two daughters: Irena and Ivanka. We all get along well with each other, but best with Zdenka, whom Dragica loves very much.

They all respected me, because they saw that I was a hard-working man, who created a great deal using his hands and his knowledge. I showed everyone that there are great people, warm friendships, and much generosity amongst us Roma in Gorica; and also that we can be socially progressive, cultured, and educated not only about our own country, but even the world beyond.

I would say that I am a friend and helper to all working men. I do not like disorder, theft, fraud, or any other chaotic or illegal business. I respect men who are hardworking and honest.

I also educate my children well. They are the most clever children in Gorica. I wish upon them all blessings and protection from the evil charms of those who would harm them.

Whenever I read this journal entry of his, I feel overwhelmed with love
for our father, who cared for us with such devotion… yet I cannot
help but also feel a rush of unease, remembering how he often went
overboard. He had specific expectations about everything we did,
especially once we became teenagers. Everything had to be the way
he wanted, and out of respect, we obeyed. Not until adulthood did
we manage to escape from his tight control…

In our house, we always went to bed early. At 7pm in the evening,
the *sinija* was set for dinner. Dining from a *sinija* was a Muslim custom.
It's a round table with short legs, ours was made of plywood, and we
all sat around it cross-legged on the floor.

We always had to keep our backs straight, and we always ate in
silence. Talking and laughing during dinner, when father was present,
was forbidden. Father was worried that we would choke from food
crumbs going down the wrong way. Proper behaviour also dictated
that one does not talk with their mouth full. Normally we would have
an hour to eat, study our assigned sura from the Qur'an, wipe off
and put away the *sinija*, and clean up by sweeping up the crumbs and
washing the dishes.

Crumbs were never left on the floor. We respected our hard-earned
bread. It was said that if you don't look after your bread, if you throw
it away and walk over it, it can curse and damn you. Whenever we
failed to clean up and sweep up the bread crumbs quickly enough,
father would tell us that the crumbs screamed whenever somebody
walked over them. It was from a story he had heard from his own
parents, about a family where people never swept up their bread
crumbs and would just walk all over them constantly. One day, the
story went, the bread crumbs had enough and screamed so loudly
that the untidy family went deaf. In another version of the story, the
bread crumbs gave the father of the untidy family a stroke instead,
rendering him mute and bedridden for the rest of his life.

Father also had an explanation for why we should always wash
up the dishes after dinner. It was also another story about an untidy
family, who always left their dirty dishes in their kitchen. Evil spirits
would come at night to eat the leftovers and would bang on the dishes,
shout, and disturb the people in the neighborhood. This happened

night after night, until finally the women of the family started washing the dirty dishes after the meal. Sure enough, the evil spirits stopped coming at night, and the neighbourhood was quiet once more. These were the reason why, according to father, it was imperative that we sweep up the crumbs and wash the dirty dishes right after dinner. We believed his stories, because he also seemed to believe them.

In matters of faith, we also followed our father's lead. We celebrated Muslim holidays or *bajrams*, the Romani celebrations of St. George's day and Alidjun, along with Catholic Easter, and Christmas. Father would go to the mosque and bow in prayer, he always had the best ram in the *mahala* for Kurban Bajram; but he also went to the Church of St. Ante to light candles, and we children decorated a Christmas Tree each year and enjoyed both our presents and the new year celebration that followed.

These celebrations that were the source of so much happiness, would strangely become a source of nightmares for me, after my forced departure from the only home I ever knew in 1992. Today I try to force myself to look beyond those nightmares, and go back far enough in to remember only the happiness that I've felt as a child so long ago.

*   *   *

To our father, the most important thing was always to do good unto others, to share the fruits of his labour with those close to him and those in need of help. When he would bring us cherries, he would tell us: "Share with children of our *mahala*! Remember that whenever you have something and eat it by yourself, Allah will be displeased, and he will stop your wishes from coming true. Whereas if you share with others, Allah will reward you, and will make people favor you for your generosity."

Father was a great friend to everybody, especially his family. He wanted to be loved by everyone, because he himself loved and respect them. Too many other people's respect for him, however, was calculated. They loved him only when they stood to benefit, and took advantage of him. Father would fetch people wood and coal to last the whole winter, too often at his own expense, gave people money, gifts, even paid for tomb repairs or new gravestones and crosses. He remembered everybody's birthday, and every holiday and celebration that warranted giving others presents.

Yet if there was even the smallest of misunderstandings, or if mother went to one of her cousins to complain about his cheating, they would immediately forget about his goodness and all his help. They would call him the worst names and would damn him for his Romani ancestry. They never even hesitated to curse him this way in front of his own children. It hurt me the most when mother's cousins would curse his "*cigan* mother" in front of me. My soul ached all the more because father always accepted it all as though it was nothing.

One day I tried to talk to him about it. He looked at me and said nothing for a while. His eyes told me that it did hurt him, but he never once admitted out loud. The only thing he ever said was, "If someone throws a rock at you, give them bread in return. Don't you ever forget that, my son!"

This crudeness and disrespect caused me a lot of suffering. I was similar to my father, our pains were identical. But he was strong and proud, and willing to act as though everything was fine between him and mother's cousins. In some ways this was a strength of his. And I wanted to have that same strength. I wanted to be proud to be Romani, just like my father.

Once when I was about to start recording another one of father's "lest it be forgotten" stories, he tried to explain to me the only way he knew how: "Some people, some of your mother's cousins among them, don't want to see that I am a man who is trying hard to accomplish a great deal through only his own strength. When they look at me, they see only a Rom; and in their eyes, Roma aren't worth much at all. They even forget all the good things I have done for them... My cheeks are as dark as they perceive them, but my soul is not! It's hard everywhere for those of us with dark skin. You are lucky, my son, that you are whiter than I am; you will be able to accomplish much more in life. Thanks to your fair skin, you can be successful. You will understand all this better as you get older. You will one day finish school and become somebody... but not here in Gorica."

After these sort of confessions, he would always toast with his shot glass, and the long lashes covering his blue eyes would gather tears. Then he would begin to dictate to me, "Alija, Mejra, Mešan, Rašid, Mušan, Šerif, Nura, Safija, Rabija, Ramo, Ejub Mubera, Zineta..."

Always just a list of names from his family, and nothing else.

I thought about the people that my father remembered. Many of them have died and were buried in various Muslim cemeteries, some of them with a tombstone and others without. It seemed to me that none of these people had ever accomplished anything, not for themselves, and not for the Roma. I read over the names of my mother's relatives. They were simple people too, sometimes moody and selfish, but good and caring when they had a reason to be. There was a lot of alcoholism and misery amongst them as well. I didn't want to be like either my mother's or my father's relatives. My father believed that I would achieve more in life because of my fairer complexion, and also because I was a better student than even most of our Catholic relatives. He also did his best to help me succeed.

When it came to education, father always ensured that we had the supplies we needed: books, notebooks, pens and pencils, other school supplies, and proper clothes, whether new or second-hand. " You are not orphans. My children don't need gratis books or social assistance." But he would always retreat when his presence was required at school. He never wanted to attend our parent-teacher meetings, lest our teachers find out that our father had dark skin. Father didn't want his Romani shadow to fall upon us.

"Dragica, you will go to the school for the parent-teacher meeting, because you are fair skinned. If they see me, they'll give our children bad marks. When I went to school, they always said, 'For *Cigani*, it is good enough to get a 2.' Maybe I too could have accomplished a lot more in life, if they didn't always tell me that."

This was a story though that father never allowed us to hear until we were much older. He didn't want to burden us. Instead, he made it clear that we were special, and that we were capable of achieving more than others."

Schooling

When we were children, I always thought in terms of our being a plurality; we Derviš Tahirović's daughters. But as time passed, I started feeling ever more lonely in that plurality. It appeared to me that I was the only one with ambitions to accomplish something more with my life, the only one who really wanted to become somebody.

Or, at least, I didn't want to have a life like my mother, or my aunts, or any other women in Gorica. But there wasn't anybody who could advise me how to make this dream of mine come true.

In elementary school, I wasn't any different from the other children. We all had the same school uniform covering our clothes, and our teachers rewarded my knowledge and accomplishments with good grades the same way they did for everyone else. I never heard the phrase, "For Cigani, it is good enough to get a 2." Even the rabble from the lower *mahala* eventually stopped waiting for us on our way to school.

But with each passing day, I could feel an abyss growing ever wider between me and my parents. Father continued to make enough money to not only provide for us, but also to keep improving and expanding our house. But his approach to our education consisted only of "you must nevers" and our dictations. He never inquired about our needs or wants, nor even our thoughts. And mother wasn't at all interested in issues concerning womanhood, perhaps because she didn't want us growing up either. She never even spoke to any of us about our periods, much less how to deal with them.

Studying and reading were my ways of escaping from reality; but there was never much for either. There was always work to do around the house, whether it was washing laundry at the fountain, be it summer or winter, washing the daily mountain of dishes, or the general maintenance of cleanliness in the house.

While we were in the first and the second grades, our mother would help us with our homework, but beat us if we received bad grades. Then, at some point, she stopped helping with our homework, but continued her beatings. We would get hit for errors in our home-work as well as pretty much everything else that went wrong during the day.

*   *   *

It was never quiet or peaceful in Gorica; there were always either celebrations or quarrels, and often both were happening at the same time. When I couldn't go to the Turbe because of the rain or the cold, I would crawl into the corner with a book, to sit and read underneath the picture of my grandfather Alija. Looking at that picture was comforting, it always gave me the feeling that someone was watching over me. But mother would soon enough find some duty or another for me to do, and would force me to leave my temporary safe haven.

How I hated those "women's duties"! Father was always understanding, and proud of his Dinda who was a good student. When he saw me with a book in my hands, he would tell my mother: "Dragica, don't disturb her! Let her study!" But he was rarely home, and mother never hesitated to assign me yet another task.

In elementary school, our Serbo-Croatian teacher, Ms. Marija Maja Miletić, was my favourite. I was fascinated by the use of language in the books she gave us to read, because it was so different from how we spoke in our *mahala.Is this correct* Our teacher brought warmth into the classroom and the wonderful literature she gave us to read brought new feelings into our souls. I always read every book our teacher assigned us, as every one of them opened a new world for me.

I also loved my teacher's recurring question: "What was the book's message?" I enjoyed analyzing novels and writing essays. It was my way of proving to the other children that I was somebody. When I used words to express my feelings, I had the impression that it a sort of creative game of imagination. And for me, this was the most magnificent way to play in the world."

Though I loved literature, I wasn't afraid of mathematics or physics either. I used to daydream about graduating from a Mechanical Technical School. I never thought about going to a regular high school or about studying the soft sciences at some prestigious University. I only wanted to become a mechanical engineer, thinking that I would always be able to find work, and would never have difficulty putting food on the table.

*   *   *

Sometimes, when women visited my mother, I would talk about my plans of wanting to pursue schooling, and the future I planned for myself. They would all look at me in awe, as if to ask: "Is it possible? Could a Romani woman receive such schooling?"

Often on those occasions, my aunt Anđa, who was so good to us in most other ways, would explain to me why I shouldn't dream so big. She always made fun of me, and for every success I had in school, she would just say "Come now, you should know that you won't get far! *Cigani* can never make it far from the pond."

She didn't believe that I could get anywhere in life, even with my good grades. She would say to me, to imply she thought I was a loudmouth: "First jump over the pond, then say 'hop'!"

Sometimes, our neighbor, the old Nura Tahirović, would tell us fairy tales about the Roma. Nura's fairy tales had their Kings and Princesses, but she was also fond of crafting happy endings for her stories' Romani beauties, with whom Kings and Princes all too often fell madly in love.

Anđa, on the other hand, always told much uglier stories, whose main purpose often seemed to be to show us that we shouldn't aim high, because we were just "*Cigani*" with "*cigan* habits". As if sensing how much her stories irritated and frustrated me, she would repeat them over and over again:

"Once upon a time, there was a beautiful *Cigan* girl. An Emperor came to like her very much, and took her away from her parents. He brought her to his kingdom and made her into a princess. But the Emperor was often away traveling, leaving her alone in the palace. One day, the Emperor returned from one of his journeys earlier than expected, and rushed into her room. And there, he saw his princess dressed like a *Cigan*, walking around from room to room and begging, 'Give me some money, good people! Give me some money!" The Emperor became furious and chased her out of the palace, saying: 'Go where you please, and do as you've learned at home.'"

I didn't understand auntie Anđa. She was a member of our family who loved us and would keep one eye on us when our parents were away from home. She herself was among those protected by my father. But she couldn't look upon my schooling without responding malice and belittling my achievements. She verbalized the unspoken opinion of many people around me, that I had no right to even wish to be anything other than what I was. This, I could never forgive her.

I always hoped to find someone who would respect my dreams and help me toward achieving them. To our surprise, one day Anđa and uncle Stari divorced, and our uncle married another Serbian woman called Duška, who was good-hearted and kind to us. Not only did Duška finally give uncle his heir, a son called Jasmin, but she managed to keep him too, and they grew old together happily.

*   *   *

After graduating from my elementary school with distinction, I applied to a Mechanical Technical School. Then, destiny interfered. My sister Jasminka, whose marks were lower, was rejected from every school. Father had foreseen the possibility, and had been looking for another way to further her education. Finally, through some connections, he managed to get my sister into the Textile Technical School. And that in itself was wonderful enough, as far as I was concerned.

But then father decided that both I and my sister should attend the same school... and with his sudden pronouncement, he block me from my dreams even as they were finally within my reach. I will never forget his words: "Let's go, children! Get ready to register! Dinda, you will withdraw your application from the Mechanical Technical School, and apply instead to the Textile Technical School. That way, you can continue study together."

My father saw nothing wrong with his decision. He had found a way for both his daughters to study something useful for their future—but he didn't much care what it was. I couldn't oppose his decision, because I didn't have the courage to beg him to change his mind. But I felt embarrassed, and trembled and cried. He could see how his decision was affecting me. Through my eyes, I sought help from my mother, but she just kept silent.

My head hurt, my ears rang, and I thought I would faint. I had to get into the car to carry my father's plan through. HE had this stern, sullen look on his face. No one could talk to him during times like that. I was so ashamed for being such a coward, and for fearing his reaction so much.

After driving us to the Mechanical Technical School, father told us, "Go now, and fetch your papers. Cancel your registration, and tell them you will go to another school!" I had to obey, and I did. As I climbed up the stairs to the Registrar's Office, many thoughts raced through my mind. I kept hoping that I would somehow be saved in the last moment. "Please give me back my registration papers. I want to attend another school." I said in a strange voice. I was hoping that the clerk would tell me that it was impossible, that I was already registered with their school. But no such luck; the man searched the files and handed me my documents. "Here you go. Best of luck with your future studies!" No one saved me, and my father was waiting for me outside.

I felt like my world had just collapsed around me. Why did my father get to make this decision for me? Did I not deserve to choose the school that I would attend? So what if that sister of mine couldn't register at the same school? If she had only studied harder, things would have been different! Why couldn't my father see how this was affecting me? Why did my mother not interfere? Why did the Romani girls in Anḓa's fairy tales have to remain beggars?

There had been no escape from my father's decision. He took us to the school, and registered us both. He registered my sister to do textile studies, and me to do chemical studies. My grades were initially very poor, just to spite my father. But soon enough, my desire to study and reach toward a better future returned.

*   *   *

Once it had become clear that I wouldn't get to study mechanical engineering, I focused once more on literature. I read mostly classics, but also fairy tales. In real fairy tales, princesses always remained princesses and married happily at the end. They were never chased out like beggars, as in auntie Anḓa's cruel tales about Romani girls.

We had a great teacher who strived to motivate students to challenge themselves by reading and studying more and more. Thanks to his own interest in journalism, he even started offering special extracurricular journalism classes to interested students. I immediately joined.

I was fortunate to have ended up with this teacher, because he recognized my potential, and encouraged me to embrace my ambitions. There were only three of us in his extracurricular class, and he introduced us to world of journalism, told us to read newspapers, listen to radio news, and watch television news reports with open ears and eyes, then summarize it all. He would direct us to focus on "the who, what, when, where, how, and why" to ensure that our information was complete.

He also taught us how to properly read our news stories, by practicing with a microphone. Our assignment was to create 10 minutes of news programming from events within our own school. These were dearly cherished moments for me in that school, though I still hadn't forgotten that I was there against my will.

Unfortunately it wasn't long before our teacher was offered another position as an editor at Radio Sarajevo. I wished him luck, not yet knowing that I would meet him again later in my life. His departure at the time was a great loss, as he always praised me, and told me that it must have been a fluke that I even ended up in his school. He thought I should have gone to a more academically focused high school that better matched my ambitions.

*   *   *

I couldn't admit to anyone that the only reason I was going go that school was because my father made me. He still had complete control over us. Looking back, I can now understand his fears, but at the time his tyranny was unbearable. My mother used to tell us how in her childhood she had to do everything to her father's wishes, down to the boots she wear and the style of her hair. I didn't have to wear large rubber boots by then, but I still had to obey my father.

He even chose the path we had to take to school and back. The school was on Dolac Malta, and father made us walk over the Railway Station. It wasn't because we didn't have money for streetcar tickets, but because he always wanted to know exactly where we were. He worried about us a great deal, as many horrible things used to happen to Romani girls. People believed that the Roma sold their own children. Or perhaps it was just a joke—if so, it was a very crude one. It was more likely their way of offending and belittling people different from themselves. Maybe our father would have been different, had he not been regularly exposed to such talk.

On the one hand, he would tell us to take pride in ourselves. "You are not peasants. You are my Sarajevan Romani girls! It's easy to spot peasant girls; their feet are wide apart, and their heels are dry and cracked. Proper ladies walk with their feet close together and hold their heads up high. The best way to master such ladylike walk is to practice with a book on your head." he would advise. And so we learned to walk like a lady with a book on our head.

But on the other hand, he never let us dress nicely, lest we attract the attention of some lecherous man. I was always so envious of all my school friends. Even those who came from remote areas and smaller villages would always have nicer and more modern dresses and shoes than ours. Knowing how to walk like ladies never quite made up for everything else.

The taxi-stop where my father worked was located at the new railway station. We passed by there every day on our way to school, so he could see us and make sure that we were "on the right path". But for all his precautions, there were still those who look upon us with ill intentions.

One day, shortly after we had gotten home, we heard the sound of father rushing in through the door, shouting our names even before he got inside. He was red in the face and beside himself, demanding from our mother whether all his daughters had arrived home safely. He told her that some idiots at the taxi stop saw us walking by, and realizing that we were his daughters, they called him a *"Cigan"*, and told him to name his price for his daughters. He told them that he was a Sarajevan Roma, and that no one in his family had ever sold their daughters. He told them that Sarajevan Romani children were free to choose their future, and that his daughters went to school.

Of course, none of that mattered to his antagonist. He refused to tell us what happened next, but it seemed clear enough that he had started a fight and placed himself in harm's way to try prove that we were different. I felt bad for him, and I understood his concerns. But his control over seemingly every aspect of our lives still made me miserable.

It would be a long time before I would see how my sisters' own choices impacted them, and gain an adult understanding of how my father really did have our best interests in mind. Though he did restrain us in many ways, he also tried to give us some sense of liberty and independence as we got older. He encouraged us to earn our allowance by washing the car, digging in our garden, or assisting with various chores around the house. And when he handed us our money, he would always tell us, "Here, this is *your* money! You can buy yourself cola or whatever else at school or when you go out. You don't have to go out with boys, and allow them to kiss you or touch to just to get drinks or other things. You've earned your money; you may spend it as you please!" We didn't understand why he said what he said at the time; my sisters and I just wanted to get away from him and his smothering control.

*   *   *

In those days, I would often seek reprieve at grandma Ankica's. She lived close to our school, so I would go to her place during school breaks and after school. After uncle Antun's passing, grandma had the entire single-room apartment for herself. Since she lived on the ground floor, she had thick rods on the windows as protection from thieves. She was always clean, and smelled like apples and vanilla. Grandma's entire world was found in that room, including her kitten, her photographs, and promotional badges of her favorite soccer club. Grandma Ankica was an avid Željezničar soccer club fan, who collected anything and everything that had the symbol of the team.

Even when she wasn't at home, I would always find food left for me in a covered container in the fridge. It was the love and the care of my grandmother that helped me to survive the most trying times of my childhood.

Father continued to have ever reason to be proud of my academic achivements. I completed high school as a straight A student. And this time, my father and I did talk about how my studies should progress. He, of course, had his own ideas about what I should do with my life. He insisted that I enroll in law school, but I was not keen on it.

I felt brave and told father about my own idea; I wanted to study in Belgrade to become a playwright. The mere idea enraged my father! "No way!" he shouted, "Only girls with loose morals leave home to go live in another city by themselves. Actresses and other indecent women, what business have you got with such people?!" And so once more, I had to be "a proper Sarajevan Romani girl", obey father, and study criminology.

I didn't give up completely though, and I chose fields of study that were unavailable in Sarajevo. The only university that offered the programs I chose was located in Zagreb. When I told father, he started angrily criticizing my mother, though she had nothing to do with any of it. He said it was her fault for raising me this way. He said that if

I went to study in another city, he would publicly renounce me and disown me.

When he spoke those words, both I and my mother began to sob. I didn't know whether mother was crying out of compassion for me or because she was being unjustly accused; but there was nothing else women could do but to cry and to obey the decisions made by men. My attempts to escape that house and that way of life proved futile. Perhaps one of the reasons I later feared going to places by myself was because I had gotten so used to my father fighting to protect us. I would came to hate myself for being such a coward.

Despite submitting to my father's demands, I continued to have a craving for freedom. I dreamed of finding an apartment where I could live alone, even while maintaining my ties with my family. As unyielding as he may have been, I did need him in my life.

My high school diploma allowed me to find a job right away. I got a job as a fabric technician in a dry cleaning facility, working at various locations, wherever additional workers were needed.

I performed various tasks, ranging from transporting clothing between different facilities, to working on expense reports. My bosses soon realized that I had a talent for doing calculations, as mathematics was a strength of mine, so they started giving me more and more such work. I remember some of my supervisors quite fondly. Mrs. Zarifa from the branch-office "Svetozar Marković" was the head supervisor; yet, she and I often engaged me in stimulating conversations. She saw that I was capable of being more than just a chemical technician. Soon enough, as both my coworkers and management got to know me, I found myself received with open arms wherever I was assigned. And since all the offices were accessible by streetcar, I also had the pleasure of frequent rides throughout the city.

And so for the first time in my life, I was earning my own living. But it still didn't bring me the freedom I desired. At the end of the month, I had to hand in my salary and my pay stubs to my father; such was the unwritten rule. Children had to give back to their parents at least part of what they had invested in them. And my father continued to demand my obedience, the same way as when I was a child.

I needed more freedom, and the only way toward it that I could see was through University. I inquired about various educational programs, and found that journalism appealed to me. The profession fundamentally involved movement from place to place and was beyond the reach of the our *mahala* and my father's worrying. So I went to write the entrance exam, which I didn't find difficult at all, thanks to my prior focus writing and literature. The idea of journalism as a profession was looking better all the time, and I eagerly awaited the results of my exam.

*   *   *

The day when the results were announced, I went to 70 Skenderija street, the Faculty of Political Studies and Political Science in Sarajevo, where the department of journalism was located. The lists of accepted candidates were displayed at the entrance and I checked each lists over and over again, but I couldn't find my name anywhere. Tears welled up in my eyes, blurring my vision. How could this be? Am I really such a failure? People stared at me, as I quietly said goodbye to my dreams.

There was a part of me, however, that refused to accept that I couldn't pass what had seemed like a fairly easy entrance exam. So I decided to double-check by going directly to student services, albeit with tears continuing to roll down my cheeks. I already started thinking that I would simply have to try elsewhere.

Finally reaching the clerk, I told her, "I'm Hedina Tahirović and my name is not on the list of the students that have been accepted. I would like to get my application documentation back." But this time turned out to be different from four years earlier at the Mechanical Technical School. The clerk looked at me, searched for my documents, then suddenly told me, 'But you are accepted! Congratulations!'" The shock of this news only multiplied my tears, but now I was crying from joy, realizing that I had made a breakthrough. I had taken my first real step toward attaining the freedom I so desired.

I did my best to mentally prepare myself for the challenge of studying and working at the same time. When I attended my first lecture, I felt like I was in heaven. I beamed with pride, knowing that I was the first woman from Gorica to ever to get into University. As the professor called out each student's name during attendance check, he paused at my name.

"Hedina Tahirović?"

"Present," I said, rising from my chair.

"Thank God, we have a girl from Sarajevo!", he told me, then moved on.

I felt like I was twelve feet tall! Not only had I passed the entrance exam; I was also accepted as being simply a Yugoslavian girl from Sarajevo. For a Romani girl, that seemed like a very special accomplishment.

My time at the university lasted for only five years of my life, but it seemed like an eternity. As my growing burdens and responsibilities started weighing more heavily on me, it seemed as though I nearly stopped living in the present altogether, and instead focused only on my one major goal: graduating from university. Without that single-minded focus, I'm not sure I would've gotten through that period of my life.

*   *   *

In another attempt to sever myself from my father's authority, and rush towards an imaginary freedom that didn't exist; I married a man, whom I loved very much. Youthful romanticism sees life through rose colored glasses. And so it was, that I exchanged my father's smothering protection for my husband's and his family's unfamiliar care.

After we married, I soon gave birth to a child, and almost immediately thereafter my husband was called in to do his mandatory military service. I was left alone in my late mother-in-law's half-finished house, whose concrete walls seemed impossible to ever properly warm up.

Those Sarajevo winters were brutal. During the Olympic games, the meter high snow on the ground made for a downright magical experience for the tourists; but for those without enough firewood, they were terrible times. Oftentimes even the inside walls would come to be covered with frost.

The one thing I never had difficulty with was studying. Even in the most difficult situations, I found temporary refuge from my problems in my books. I would sit on the floor, and rock my child on my stretched legs. We both needed each others, and I knew my son to be intrinsically mine, still in his own way a part of me, and an incredible source of strength.

I would rock him back and forth, even as the book in my hands would rock with the same rhythm. My eyes quickly got used to reading such swinging letters, and I always read out loud. My son found comfort in my voice, and it helped him to fall asleep. But as I stopped reading and rocking him on my legs, he would wake up and start crying.

Awakened by his cries, I would start rocking him anew, and would resume reading for the both of us, so that I could stay longer in the world of my books, and my son could sleep. Whenever my voice had completely faded, I woke up, the same as my child, and found myself back in reality, and completely alone.

*   *   *

I was usually alone during my husband's military service. Even as I was studying for my exams, I was never sure whether I would be able to buy milk the next day. What's more, as a result of circumstances beyond my control, I had lost my job too.

At night, I would often travel the road between Širokača, where I lived, and my father's house in Gorica. He forgave me for marrying without his approval, and for running away from home. My mother, on the other hand, interpreted my actions as being a complete, final, and irreversible departure. She felt that I had made my choice, and that my life and my problems were no longer their concern. She became even more cold and distant, and occasionally behaved with cruelty towards me. Perhaps she would have been a different woman, had she lived her life under different circumstances.

Sometimes during these troubled times, Father would say, "Alright, my son, we will help you," only for mother to intervene and say, "No, I will not help her!" Her rejection in those moments felt horrible. I remember one time when I had asked my parents to watch my son for me, so that I could go to write my exam. Mother stayed silent and avoiding my gaze, clearly I couldn't count on her to babysit for me. Eventually my father told me, "I will look after him, leave him with me." He knew how important this exam was for me. But mother got angry with him, "No, Derviš! You're just going to go to work, and the burden of caring for the child will once more fall on my shoulders. I don't want these obligations anymore!"

Hearing her words, I just stood there in front of them, feeling hurt and humiliated. I realized that if I left my son with my father, they would get into a fight; and I didn't want that. Staring down at the ground in front of me, I told my father, "It's ok, Tata. I'll manage somehow..."

Trying to hold back my tears, I left my parent's house and returned home to Berkuša. I sat and rocked my son, while reading to him as he came to expect. When the time came for me to go, I took my baby with me to my exam. Thankfully, some fellow students on a different exam schedule agreed to look after him while I wrote my exam. Once finished, I went back home. It was several days later that I learned I had passed my exam, despite how distraught I had been while writing it.

After this incident, I vowed to never again visit my parents or seek their help. But after a while, I would become homesick and forget about my mother's harsh treatment. Whenever I would come by, she would greet me with a smile, welcome me into the house, and offer me coffee—but nothing more. She refused to listen to me talk about my life and my ambitions to graduate despite my challenges. She would counter me with harsh words, telling me, "Life is the way it is! You chose the man you married, you should take care of him now!" I envied women who could still find shelter in their parents' home after getting married, and it hurt me a greatly that it wasn't the case for me.

*   *   *

I want to remember the good things as well, especially those that I had my father to thank for. We created a whole new ritual when my father first cut my son's hair. My Edis, known affectionately as Kiki, was his grandpa's godchild too. In the early morning of April 8th, 1983, at Kiki's first birthday, my parents, and my brother Alin knocked on my door. My husband was still in the military service in Vukovar, but he was by then serving his last few days.

Father had brought a present for Kiki. They entered the house, reciting the Bismillah prayer. Father asked me to gather a tray, a comb, a pair of scissors, and a glass of water.

Once he had everything, he put some coins in the glass of water, and took my son into his arms. My brother Alin carried a tray with some special objects required for the ceremony, while mother and I followed behind them. We left my house, and walked towards the small bridge in Berkuša *mahala*, close to the home of Davlija Palo. As we reached the bridge, my father started reciting suras as prayers from the Qur'an, and he took the comb, dipped it in the water, and combed Kiki's hair. Then he grabbed the scissors, and cut the long hair from his forehead, then from the side of his head, continuing to pray even as he cut each lock of hair.

When finished cutting, father placed the hair into the glass of water. He instructed me to let the hair soak for a day, and then place the hair in a cloth and let it dry. A child's first cut locks had to be kept as a talisman. I followed father's instructions, and some days later I placed the wrapped up hair into my son's pillow. According to Romani beliefs, those first cut locks of hair hold magical powers and guard the child throughout his life from evil eyes, witches, and nightmares.

Looking back now, I have greater appreciation of my father. He helped me and my family during the heavy winter the year of the Olympics. When we had to abandon our house, he let us stay in his basement, where so many others in need had stayed before us. Had he not opened his arms, and provided us shelter, I might never have completed my university studies. But with his help, though it was still difficult, I came up with inventive ways of financing my education, knowing that I would ultimately succeed.

Here are some more of entries from my father's notebook. He wrote these in his own hand. They describe the world as he saw it, always better than it really was.

Journal Entry by Derviš Tahirović, 1983.

This year, my wife Dragica and I experienced immense sadness. My wife's sister Zdenka, whom she loved dearly, has passed away. Zdenka left two children behind. She had just moved into a new apartment and had not even bought her furniture. She lied down and never got up again. Poor Zdenka!

Dragica lost her sister, and I lost my brother Ramo. He died in my house the same way as cousin Rašid had died... Alcohol destroyed them both.

Before he died, my brother became delirious, and saw ghosts around him. He even saw a man in the oven, and he was convinced the man wanted a cigar. In his delusional state of mind, Ramo kept screaming: "Look at his head, it's like the head of cabbage. Here, take the cigar and smoke it!" And with these words, He would take a cigar out of the box and throw it into the oven. His strange behavior frightened the childrenl.

  Alcohol is a horrible thing. Many good men die from its abuse.

Journal Entry by Derviš Tahirović, January 26, 1984.

I would like to appeal to every real Bosnian and Yugoslavian, regardless of their faith, to unite for the organization of the 1984 Winter Olympiad due to take place on February 8th in our beloved city of Sarajevo.

  The reader and interpreter of these words, who will one day read my notebook, should understand that the Olympic Games are organized in the noblest spirit of brotherhood and the equality of all peoples of Bosnia and Herzegovina and all of Yugoslavia. And so we must all guard our city from wrongdoings that could destroy such a historical event!

  Many nations envy us because of these Olympic Games, and these enemies would strip us of this honour, given half a chance. And to them, I say, that all the inhabitants of Sarajevo and Bosnia and Herzegovina are ready to prevent any and all incidents, and will respond tenfold as strong to their attacks!

  Anybody wanting to ruin the Olympic Games for us will be sorry, because we are ready to defend it!

Journal Entry by Derviš Tahirović, 1984.

I want to write about something positive now. The Gala night will be remembered and recorded in the Romani history of this city! The "Romani Ball" was held in Sarajevo's Hotel Europe, with our most famous singer's and their musicians in attendance: Sulejman Ramadan Ramče, Sejdi Sejdi, and Nečko Esadović.

  The Art & Culture association "Alija Hodžić" from Gorica also participated, with their choreographers Cota and Nuno, and Romani activist Fadil Sejdović, my half-sister Rabija's half-brother. Several of our family members were also in attendance. My daughter Elvira is a member of the association and participated in the Bosnia and Herzegovina pageant. She was selected as the most beautiful Romani girl! I was also present, though I did not take active part in any of the activities.

  This was the most beautiful and most magnificent night of my life. In front of two thousand people, my daughter was crowned Miss Roma 1984!

As her father, I was very proud of her and extremely happy. In fact, perhaps the word "happy" is not even accurate I was more than happy! My closest friends created a magnificent atmosphere, singing and dancing until dawn.

All the Roma sang and danced as never before right until the daylight returned. People say there hadn't been such a magnificent celebration in the last ten years. I would like to emphasize that in our Yugoslavia, Roma obtained full affirmation and full rights alongside the other nationalities: the Serbs, the Muslims and the Croats. I wish to emphasize that we all have equal rights, and I desire for it to remain so in the future too!

Journal Entry by Derviš Tahirović, Autumn, 1985.

Nobody is happier than I am today! In 1985, my daughter Hedina graduated from the Faculty of Political Sciences of Veljko Vlahović in Sarajevo with a degree in journalism. She is married to Rahiz Sijerčić, and they have a three year old son Edis, whose first locks of hair I had cut. Hedina is my pride and joy. Thank God that one of us is accomplishing something with their life by completing University. My daughter made it! Hats off to her!

*   *   *

I remember very well how proud of me my father was. On the day that I brought home my diploma, I had my small revenge on aunt Anđa, who was visiting us. I took out the diploma from its red case to show my father. He hugged me, and I could see a tear forming in the corner of his eye. Seeing all this, my aunt just sat there with her mouth agape and her eyes wide; she was speechless.

She didn't even congratulate me, just sat there with her face was burning red from shame. I felt triumphant, as I waved my diploma in front of her eyes. I didn't need her congratulations. My only words to her were, "Today Rom jumped over the pond, and now says 'hop'!"

She stared at me in silence, no doubt remembering her goading that my words echoed. Father taught us to respect our elders, but for that moment, I could not restrain myself. I wanted her to know how offensive her words had been. And once I had said my piece, I felt better right away.

*   *   *

My father had heard about an initiative at Radio-Television Sarajevo to start a program for Roma in their own native language. Only a month had passed since my graduation, and I didn't have any plans for the future yet, when he called and asked me to visit him. I rushed to my parent's house, sensing that the news was something that would prove important to me.

When I got there, I couldn't help but notice that everything looked the same. Father's car was parked on the streets and the front door was open as usual. It was the same Gorica, the same *mahala* that I remembered from my childhood. The only difference was that I was now a grown woman, who had a diploma, and a baby in her arms.

Father greeted me in the doorway with open arms. He took my son Kiki into his arms, and led me into the house. "Sit down, my son, I have to talk to you. My good friends Coto and Nuno, the activists and choreographers of the Art & Culture association of Gorica, told me that Radio-Television Sarajevo has an opening for a journalism graduate. The person they hire will produce a program in Romani. Apparently, it's not a problem if you don't speak Romani yet, you could learn enough of the language in time for the first broadcast. A journalist named Radmilo Bato Zurovac approached our friends Coto and Nuno to ask them if they knew of an educated Roma that could do the job. What do you think about this, my son? Tell me, Dinda, would you be ashamed to publicly say that you are Romani woman?"

I looked at my father for a few moments in disbelief. Why was he asking me such a thing? When had I ever ceased to be a Romni? Even as I failed to fight back by tears, I told him, "Tata, I am not ashamed of you! I am the same as you, I am Romni like Thunder! I am proud of your heritage because it is also mine. I understand things a lot better than when I was a child. I understand that true freedom is being free to say who you are, and being free to do what you love."

*   *   *

When the opening was announced, I applied, and was called in for testing soon enough. It was then that I first met Radmilo Bato Zurovac, my future mentor. The test had written and oral components in both Romani and Serbo-Croatian. There were very few of us taking the test, but my knowledge of Romani was very poor.

I had spent a few weeks preparing for the test in our *mahala*, gathering information about the events in Gorica. Thankfully, my neighbor Hajra Sejdić knew Romani very well, so she helped me develop a limited vocabulary list that I could reasonably learn and would be helpful for the test. I learned a few important expressions by heart, and I practiced them over and over again. Thankfully, Romani had always been spoken around me, and so I had no problem with the pronunciation.

Once the written portion of the test was completed, we were asked to read out what we wrote in Romani and in Serbo-Croatian. I took a seat in front of the studio microphone and suddenly noticed across the table my old high school Professor. He waived at me, looking surprised. It seemed like he was confused, and didn't understand what I was doing among these Romani applicants. Perhaps he couldn't believe that I was a Romni.

He walked closer to greet me, and addressed me by my maiden name, Tahirović. At that time, I had already taken on my married name, Sijerčić; but I was very happy that someone was calling me by my maiden name, that they remembered me from so long ago. He encouraged me by telling me I would surely succeed. He reminded me that I had always read well and spoke well since the time of his journalism classes. And he was right, I did do very well! In fact I had no real competition, as I was the only one with a University degree.

Afterwards, I was reassured that my limited knowledge of Romani would not be a problem, as long as I was willing to learn. And in the following weeks, I received notice that I had been chosen for the position of the planned Romani program's producer. I immediately received two collaborators, two announcers who spoke perfect Romani: Gordana Sejdić, who spoke Gurbeti, and Ramadan Gani, who spoke the Arlia dialect.

Working as a journalist 1985-1992: Spring 1986.
My first broadcast

All the peoples of the former Yugoslavia shared the same destiny for five centuries, in being ruled by foreign governments. Slovenes and Croats were ruled by the Austro-Hungarian Empire. Serbs, Macedonians, Bosniaks, and Montenegrins were ruled by the Ottoman Empire. For most of that time, there were few schools and people generally lacked literacy in their own mother tongue.

Mandatory schooling was only introduced when the Kingdom of Yugoslavia was formed after World War I. In the countries of the former Yugoslavia, education for women became available only when Tito and the communists came into power. Croats, Serbs, and Bosniaks had all attained an enviable level of literacy and education in a mere 60 years. In that short span, many great literary works were born in Yugoslavia, and many more jewels of world literature and science were translated into Serbo-Croatian. The first high school in Sarajevo opened only in 1945, but by the eighties the city was an academic centre for its region and beyond.

It was only the Roma, who remained objects instead of subjects of this revolution. Movies were made about them, old and contemporary music was played and modeled after their songs. Yet all they had was their centuries old traditions and the hostility of the non-Roma surrounding them, which worked to keep them poor and illiterate.

Eventually, the government of Bosnia and Herzegovina opened its eyes to this social crisis. Their attempted remedy was to pay more attention to their national minorities, especially the Roma, and place greater emphasis on their education and integration. One part of that plan was the establishment of my Romani language radio program. And to emphasize its political significance, I and the other producers decided to make our first show a very special live broadcast.

In preparation for my new job, I undertook a short internship at Belgrade's Studio B. I participated in the production of the Romani radio show "Ašunen Romalen", whose editor Dragoljub Acković was himself a Rom. That program had already been running for a number of years and had many listeners. It was there that I learned how to moderate discussions, and also improved my already respectable microphone and radio skills.

After my internship was over, I myself prepared the script determining who will say what and when, during our first broadcast. My mentor, Bato Zurovac merely checked through my work to make the occasional correction. I had left left nothing to chance, not even my wardrobe. My old neighbors in Gorica were so overjoyed to having one of their own hosting a television show that they lent me a beautiful white traditional Romani costume.

We titled our radio show "Lačho djive, Romalen", intending "Romalen" to refer to all Yugoslavians, whether Roma or Gadžo. The first broadcast aired in the Spring of 1986, straight from the hotel "Bosna" in Ilidža, and I was its host and editor. We had several high profile guests: Hamdija Pozderac, a highly ranked politician in Bosnia and Herzegovina; Dr. Milan Šipka, a linguist who worked at the Institute for Observation of National Minorities; Rajko Đurić, the President of Yugoslavian Roma; and Sait Balić, the President of the International Romani Union. We also had Esma and Stevo Teodosievsky's group "Sulejman Ramadan Ramče" on our show, whose tours took Romani music around the world, and several editors of already established Romani radio and television programs in Belgrade, Priština and Skopje.

Though my father drove me to the the "Hotel Bosna" that day, he didn't stay. He said that he had to work that night, but I knew the real reason was that he was afraid I wouldn't feel free to speak my mind if he were around. In this way, my father could often be very attentive to my needs.

There was also another man to whom I owe a great deal; the renowned editor of Radio Sarajevo, Radmilo Bato Zurovac. He introduced our program that first day, then me as its host and editor-in-chief, and Gordana and Ramadan as its anchors. He also explained that I was the first Romani journalist in the history of Radio-Television Sarajevo, and gave me a microphone as a gift, as a symbol of my new vocation with the station.

The show was a success and went off without any glitches. People from the media photographed and reported on the event. After the show ended, Zurovac gave me a more personal introduction to the politicians. Hamdija Pozderac offered me the seat next to him, shook my hand, and said to me, "*Aferim*! Bravo, my son!"

*   *   *

After that first show, I kept hearing that congratulatory *aferim* again and again. In my Gorica, mother would turn on the radio, cranking the volume as high as she could, and all our neighbors would come out to listen. My mother actually knew the Romani language better than my father, because she spent a lot of time socializing with the other women. Not to mention a masterful use of language was crucial to the sort of fortunetelling they practiced. Father, in turn, used to listen to my show with his colleagues at the radio station. Both my parents were proud of me, and couldn't help telling anyone and everyone that their little Dina had grown up to become a journalist.

Though our first show was the first I had publicly spoken Romani, my neighbours all congratulated me afterwards. I felt that they were proud of me as somebody who was one of their own. My achievement also symbolized a renewed hope, leading people to believe once more that things would change for the better.

Of course, the process was just beginning. One of the show's goals was to increase awareness about the living conditions of Romani people. But it was impossible to create better living conditions for people in Gorica overnight, as the problems they suffered with every day had already spanned decades. When my father was a child, promises were made by politicians that the neighbourhood would be renovated, and that new houses would be built; but their promises turned out to be empty, as political pledges often do. I was aware of the reality, and I believed that if we spoke openly about the problems, the Municipal authorities would realize the need to improve conditions. In any case, the program was a huge step for us Roma.

For me, personally, it was also a dream come true, and a path toward new opportunities I've never even dreamed of. My father must have understood this as well, because he rejoiced with me. The following journal entry dates from the same period.

Journal Entry by Derviš Tahirović, May 27, 1987.

Hedina is still editor of the Romani language radio program "Lačho dijve, Romalen". I often listen to her on the radio, while waiting for my turn to take the next ride at our taxi stand. She even learned the Romani language. All my colleagues know that she is my child, my child...

*   *   *

But my father also suffered a great deal because of his daughters, whom he tried to protect his entire life. All my sisters, including me, married without regard for our father's approval over the men we chose; though in retrospect, all he wanted was to ensure our future husbands would love and cherish us as the precious women he believed us to be.

Perhaps what happened with my youngest sister Elvira hit him hardest. She left school ran away from home in 1986 and, though still underage, she married a boy she had fallen in love with. After that incident, my father had become a different man. It was though he had lost all hope that he alone could accomplish anything anymore. Maybe one day I'll find the strength to write about my sisters' destinies... but for now, let me just say that they live scattered throughout Europe. After 1986, only my youngest brother Alin had continued to live with my parents.

Thanks to the opportunities I was offered, I managed to push aside the various traumas of my childhood. I now had just one goal, a vision: I was going to become the first Romani journalist. Having found this new focus, I no longer needed any help from either my father or from any other men in my family. Journalism was now my domain and my source and means of freedom.

Of course, at that time I also had my personal duties as a mother and a wife, and had many day to day problems to deal with. But everything was now easier to handle, because I could always find reprieve in my work. When I would be talking to guests, editing the recordings, or doing other production work, those were the times when I felt like I was being my true self. I also increasingly felt that I was also a part of a great Romani nation, and having long been aware of the challenges it was facing, I really started to believe that it was possibly to affect change through the media, especially for the younger generation.

*   *   *

The Romani activists who met in Sarajevo: Slobodan Mustafović, Hedina Sijerčić, Milan Šipka, Sait Balić with an activist from Niš, Fadil Sejdović, Azem Ajvazi, Ramo Mujkić, Sunčica Findak, Rahim Burhan, Bajram Haliti with an activist from Kosovo, siting: Mehmed Saćipi

I did my first interviews with Sait Balić, the President of the International Romani Union, and with Dr. Rajko Đurić, the President of Yugoslavian Roma. Though I kept asking about education programs, both of these men were political leaders for the Roma, and primarily focused their efforts on fighting for the Roma go gain official national minority status. Problems of education they mentioned only in passing.

Language was another great challenge. Many were forgetting the language, and even more had never learned it to begin with. Worse yet, even those who did know, permitted their Romani vocabulary to be overwhelmed by Serbo-Croatian or other larger languages spoken around them. The fundamental problem as I saw it was that even the most diligent of us only used Romani in daily conversations, whereas what with needed were formal educational programs and institutions that would teach and use our language in their classes. I frequently talked about this issue in my broadcasts.

One of the first books for learning the basics of the Romani language was compiled by a Frenchman called Marcel Courthiade. His book was the only one at the time that I was aware; but he wasn't a Rom, and his book was not comprehensible to the Roma of Bosnia.

There was also another man whose work focused on the Romani language; Rade Uhlik, a scientist specializing in Romani studies, who lived right in Sarajevo. I had the pleasure of having him on one of my programs once. Talking to him was sometimes difficult, as he was already in his eighties by the time of our interview. He wasn't Rom, but he had spent a long time living among nomadic Roma in Bosnia, and Herzegovina, recording their language and their customs.

He had written a Serbo-Croatian – Romani – English dictionary, still in use today. I never stopped using it myself, as it continues to be the best dictionary available. He wrote many papers and books about the sociography and ethnography of the Roma. He also worked out a standardization of Romani, based on the Gurbeti dialect, which he believed to be the purest of all the dialects.

I received many brochures from him about his work, but I did not manage to save them, and they must have been destroyed during the way along with everything else in our apartment. I am certain though that the National Museum in Sarajevo would have a complete collection of his works. Rade Uhlik should have gotten greater international recognition, and he was a certainly a man who deserved to be remembered.

In those days, I tried to talk about anything that could inspire the spirit of our people. There were very few Romani literary works, as stories were generally passed on through oral tradition and seldom recorded. Therefore I did my best to find the few Romani authors and poets who could be sources of moving Romani writing.

The Novi Sad writer Trifun Dimić was one such person. He wrote poems and recorded folk songs in both Serbian and Romani. He was also involved in literary translation, indeed he had translated the Old and New Testaments into Romani for his local church. I interviewed him as well. Unfortunately he died very young. I recently learned that a street in Novi Sad bears his name. I am glad to know that he hasn't been forgotten.

Šemso Avdić from Banja Luka was another Romani poet who wrote and published poetry in Romani, as well as Serbo-Croatian and Italian. He became a frequent guest on our program. If he couldn't be there in person, we would read his poetry, he was so dear to us.

Though our program's target audience consisted primarily of people who were illiterate and had no technical understanding of either poetry or metaphors; they could nonetheless feel the essence of those verses, especially in poems like for example "The Vow" by Jovan Nikolić. We wanted to create an artistic experience for our listeners through poetry and music. I read that poem on air in both Serbo-Croatian and Romani, while Russian Romani instrumental music played in the background.

The Vow

Should I ever have a son,
He will go straight from his mother's breast into a cage.
I shall feed him with raw meat.
Instead of toys,
I shall give him wild animals,
So they shall sniff one another,
So they shall slaughter one another,
So that he would learn their language.
And when he attacks a cat;
He shall be ready to wed.
And when he breaks the back of a wolf,
I shall know that my labour wasn't in vain.
When he bites off my hand,
Even as I feed him;
Then, I shall let him go amongst people.

— Jovan Nikolić

Sovli

Chavo te avela man
katar pe dake chuchi an kafezo dzala

dzuvdo mas le me dava
ruvenca le thava
te sungin pe te chinen pe
lenge chib te sikljol
thaj kana pe rich hutela
vov borake pacho avela
kana kor ruveske shaj phagela
dzanava kaj mor zor ivja najsasa
kana mor chav mor va hala
o vast kaj les pravardasa
mashkar e manusha shaj vov dzala.

— Jovan Nikolić

From the collection "A guest from nowhere", published in 1981.

I also enjoyed reading poetry by Rajko Đurić, and his poem "Without a home, without a grave" is one of my favourites. It always seemed to me like these two poems, the previous one by Nikolić and this one by Đurić, have been with me my entire life.

Without a home without a grave

O-o-o I shall be miserable until the end of the days
O-o-o my dear father
You without a grave
We without a home
We are swept by winds
We are expelled by the world.

Where shall we go
How long shall we last
O-o-o mother dearest
Which stones shall we step on
Where shall we call you from

The sky has closed upon us
The land is deserted
It so appears

Where shall we go
How long shall we last
Who will get closer
Who will get further
Existence in the middle of nowhere

— Prof. Dr. Rajko Đurić

Bi kheresko bi limoresko

O-o-o lele mange sajek
O-o-o joj dade morejana
Tu bi limoresko

Amen bi kheresko
Te avas e balvalake po phurdipe
e themese po khandipe

Kaj maj
Dzikaj maj

O-o-o joj daje guglijena
Pe savo barh te achav
Katar tut te akharav
Phanglo si amenge o del
E phuv sargo kaj chuchi si
bi khanikasko

Kaj maj
Dzikaj maj

Kon pashavol
Kon duravol
Mashkar e xasarde droma trajimase

— Prof. Dr. Rajko Đurić

From the collection "Without home, without a grave", published in 1979.
Dr. Rajko Đurić was not only a politician and a poet, but also an excellent journalist, who was editor-in-chief of the cultural section of Belgrade's "Politika" newspaper. In those days, he was widely considered to be the greatest Romani poet; and I believe he is credited with the same distinction even today. He has published numerous poetry collections, including his most famous one, "Without home, without grave". But when the war broke out, he no longer felt safe, and left Belgrade. Thereafter he lived and worked in Berlin for some time.

Between 1986–1991, Dr. Milan Šipka, a frequent guest on our show, focused on attempts to standardize the Romani language and, among other efforts, he organized the Sarajevo Conference. There, he spoke at length about standardization, alongside the French linguist Marcel Courthiade. Unfortunately, standardization still hasn't been achieved to this day, primarily because none of the Roma want to compromise their own various dialects.

*   *   *

After working on "Lačho djive, Romalen" for some time, I started focusing on bringing more variety into our programming. The show was initially a 30 minutes long mosaic that included many different semi-regularly recurring pieces. Later on, thanks to all the great music we played, the diversity of our discussions, and our general popularity, the program was expanded to a full hour. Happy as we were about this acknowledgement; it wasn't easy to fill a full hour, particularly as we were so often on the road.

Our new expanded program continued to include a variety of components, but the most prominent one was the news segment. We featured the most important weekly news from Yugoslavia and the world at large, but also included news about Romani life, culture, and politics too—all of it in Romani.

Another segment of the program dealt with brief documentary segments of everyday life: In one program, Romani tradesmen would talk about the traditions behind their chosen occupations; the next program, we discussed issues concerning Romani women. My collaborators and I created programming about any relevant topic that we would learn about. We didn't work by the principle that "only bad news is good news", the way so many journalists and much of the media seemed to. In fact, we tirelessly searched for good news to report about Roma, and we didn't care whether they were famous or not.

During my youth, I encountered much poverty among our people. And when I was student, I had the opportunity to experience hardship firsthand. I somehow always found a job to get me through my lean times; and my father was also there to help me as best as he could.

It was only when I made my first documentary about the Roma, and visited their temporary shelters and meager permanent homes that I realized it was possible for people to merely exist. To have lives that didn't afford even the minimum dignity that is the birthright of every human being.

There were many people from those settlements, whom I remember fondly. Several of them were elderly men and women who had never known anything but crushing poverty, though they had worked most every day of their lives. Being a journalist who was doing research for a story did not lessen my distress over the myriad harsh destinies that seemed my people's lot in life.

*   *   *

I remember an old Rom called Alija, a self-taught umbrella maker, who spent his entire life, walking from village to village on foot, fixing umbrellas to earn money to feed his family. Even in his old age, on days that he felt well enough, we would find him on the road, repairing the umbrellas of passersby. As his children also lived in poverty, Alija did not expect them to take care of him. His wife had also passed away many years ago, he didn't even quite remember when; just that he had lived alone ever since.

Alija spent his days sitting in front of his makeshift hut, made of bricks, clay, hardboard, and tin. He was always sitting in the same spot every morning I came by, and cried like a baby. I approached him, wanting to lead him into his house, thinking that he might be drunk. But he looked at me with a sense of devastation and helplessness, and wiped off his tears. My heart ached from the sight of such vulnerable Romani seniors. As I crouched next to him, and hugged him, he started crying again, and confessed his sorrow amidst his sobs:

"My pension is missing again. The mailman says it's not there, that they must not have sent it. But I know well that he took it himself... But what can I do? Where and to whom can I go to complain, my son? Nobody believes me, nobody ever believes us!"

I could offer him no words of comfort. The idea of somebody stealing a few hundred dinars from such a destitute man was shocking in its degeneracy. What sort of human being could do such a thing? I cried with him, as I didn't know at first how I could help him. But I knew I couldn't leave him feeling so miserable, so I went to the City Hall, and asked if he could get his pension paid in a different manner, ideally in person. I was fortunate in that they trusted me, and they promised to find another way. Thankfully, soon thereafter, the old Rom Alija starting receiving his pension in full and on time.

*   *   *

Roma in the settlements of Sokolović Kolonija and Poligon on Ilidža, where we often brought food and supplies, also lived in makeshift huts. The houses were all built the same way, using materials found in landfills and along the roads. These were once nomadic Roma, who had tired of travelling. They setup these temporary settlements on what they hoped was no-man's land and have lived there since.

Most times, they were tolerated, but never really accepted by those around them. Not by their neighbours, not by the municipal government. They had no drinking water, no sewage pipes, no electricity. When it rained, mud between the huts was knee-high; when drought came, one could breathe from all the dust.

In one of the settlements, there was an old Romni called Behara, who reminded me of my grandmother Mejra. She had a light complexion and several gold teeth. I also suspect that she may not have been as old as she seemed, because she had strong legs and a sharp mind. Her long, colourful skirts swirled around her legs when she walked. When I first addressed her in Gurbeti Romani, she immediately rushed over to me and kissed me. She accepted me as one of her own, and invited me into her home for coffee.

Behara's house had a door and doorsill, but no concrete floor. Just the same dry soil found outside her house. There was an old stove in the corner, with a chimney going through the roof. Something was cooking in a dark, beat-up pot—Behara's lunch, no doubt. She placed the kettle onto the stove, and we stepped out, waiting for the water to boil. She wanted to treat me as an honoured guest, and I couldn't decline her hospitality.

She told me that she makes ends meet by begging and doing fortunetelling. She wasn't ashamed to tell me this. What else could she do, after all? Nobody would hire such an old woman! She wasn't even wanted anywhere when she was youn; and now that she was old, she had no pension. When death takes her, who knows where she will be buried. She knew this too, and told me she didn't care where her grave would be. She had no birth certificate, and would probably never be issued a death certificate either. For lack of any documentation, Behara couldn't be registered as a resident. In fact, this was a woman old enough to be my grandmother, who didn't exist on paper at all.

Once the water had boiled, she prepared the coffee, and brought it out in a kettle with two cups. We sat in front of her house, sipping coffee and chatting. She accepted her life the way it was. She saw that her situation saddened me, but she told me not to dwell on the harshness of life and poverty, as doing so only brought heartache. She explained that she didn't mind living the way she did, because once we drop dead, every last one of us goes to the other world empty-handed. And if we pass into the next world with nothing, we can live in this one much the same way.

She stroked my hair with a motherly touch, and came to comfort me instead of me comforting her. She had no bitterness about her apparent destiny and shed no tears.

As I was preparing to leave, I tried to hand her some money, but she refused. She told me that she didn't take money from our kind, only from the other kind, those who ruined her life. She said that they had to feed her until the end, and that was enough. So instead, I went to the nearby store, and bought some coffee and sugar, which she accepted with gratitude.

*   *   *

Of course, not all Roma were poor. Some people had managed to accumulate wealth through connections and business acumen, the same way as everyone else. I once visited Visoko to see how Roma lived there, and to find guests for my show. I was constantly searching for positive examples of Roma who had overcome poverty and discrimination.

As I reached the the settlement at Visoko, a man came to greet me. I knew that I had seen him before, but I couldn't remember who he was. He remembered me though, and addressed me by my name, telling me that he was a friend of my father's.

He invited me into his home, as his wife and children were eager to meet me. Only then did I finally recognize him to be Nail, who often visited us in Gorica when I was a child.

Although he was well dressed, I didn't expect his home to look like a palace. His two storey house stood out from all the other ones in town, even the more recently built ones. I paused, amazed by the grand sight. Nail was a very handy man, just like my father. He was involved in the jewelry resale business, and had a well developed network of suppliers and sellers both in Yugoslavia and abroad. And it was a family business in the most literal sense, as his wife also worked with him, and even his children joined them once they were old enough.

As a result of his hard work and ingenuity, Nail and his family lived in the world extravagance. Looking at his house, it was clear that he had commissioned the blueprints himself and imported the building materials from abroad. His doors and windows were decorated very differently than anywhere else I've ever seen. His large balconies were filled with colourful flowers in traditionally decorated Romani clay pots, and his backyard looked out onto the entire *mahala*.

I had never before been in such a beautiful home. Everything was new, clean, and thoughtfully decorated from the furniture and the carpets, to the coffee cups and saucers. Nail, noticing my awe, continued his tour by taking my upstairs. His children all had their own bedrooms, decorated with the most modern furniture.

And the bathroom! Every inch of it was covered with the most beautiful sparkling tiles, and there was an enormous sunken Jacuzzi at the centre of it. Most Bosnians built their homes using their earnings and credit, caring more about price than luxury. But Nail, in the middle of a Romani *mahala* built a palace for his family.

His home must have been the jealous envy of every successful business man from the city centre. But I was only too happy for him. It always delighted me when I found Romani stories beyond mere poverty for my programs.

*   *   *

Gordana and Ramadan, our original anchors, eventually left the program. Gordana got married, and Ramadan had left to pursue less prestigious but better paying work as a taxi driver. I was teamed up with new collaborators: Našid Spahić, Mirsad Mujkić, and Smaragda Klino. Though none of them were Roma, they all worked hard to develop meaningful and positive editorials on everyday Romani life.

At the same, I became the program's editor-in-chief, and I had also taken on job of choosing the music used in our weekly broadcasts. I played a wide variety of music including the Roma brothers Ivanovićs, Esma Redžepova, Šaban Bajramović, Raja, Volšaninov, Gordana Jovanović, Ramče, Nečko, Sejdija, the brothers Serbezovski, Muharem and Ajnur, Vida Pavlović, Amela, Zvonko Demirović, Šaban Šaulić, Keba, and others. My favourite songs were always those that whose lyrics were in the Romani language too.

I soon began to feel the power and impact that our broadcasts had. From the beginning, a bond of trust was formed between me and the various Romani groups in Bosnia and Herzegovina and beyond. Romani children would rejoice at the chance to meet me in person. And everyone, from children to adults, wanted to show convey their gratitude and respect for me. But it was always Čergaši Roma in Sokolović Kolonija and Poligon on Ilidža whom I enjoyed visiting most. They always spoke honestly about themselves, and never displayed the slightest bit malice or jealousy toward anyone else.

My work also introduced me to other sorts of activities, like organizing concerts and balls. I used to organize aid concerts in Skenderija for the benefit of Roma in Sokolović Kolonija and Poligon on Ilidža. Their living conditions really were substantially below the demands of human dignity. Nobody living in the city could imagined such poverty.

With the help of Red Cross and its activists, I organized the distribution of firewood in the winter, along with groceries, and special aid for newborns in the form of clothing, extra food, and diapers. And with the help many famous musicians, I organized Balls for the Roma.

These Balls always featured an impressive list of Romani musicians, like the famous Ramče and his brother Sejdi, the wonderful Esma Redžepova, who never tired from singing the most beautiful Romani music, and countless others, including Muharem, and Ajnur Serbezovski, Sejdi, Nečko Esadović, Medo Čun, Džekson Curik, Hasiba Agić, Subhija Šehovic, Feruz Mustafov, Gordana Jovanović, little Đore, and Fikret Ibrašimovizć and his orchestra. We also always had an equally impressive list of non-Roma musicians and artists, including Omer Livnjak, Amela Zuković, Halid Bešlić, Nazif Gljiva, Semir Cerić–Koke, my fellow radio hosts Enver Šadinlija and Mirsad Ibrić, Mirsad Sijerčić and his orchestra, Nijaz Hatić with Djokica and his

A Romani Ball in Sarajevo. Ramče and Hedina interviewing the beauties.

orchestra, Subhija Sehović, and Blagica Pavlovska. The famous actress Dora Stojiljković was one of our permanent guest, and we also frequently had the pleasure of having the poet Bisera Alikadic do readings for us.

It always warmed my heart, how quickly our illustrious roster of musicians and artists would respond to our call to donate their time and money, along with our long-standing sponsor, Zare Herceglić.

We used to hold special celebrations for the Romani New Year, organizing a beauty pageant on top of the usual festivities. We would also receive donated clothing and nylon stockings from the clothing factories "Ključ" and "ŠIK" for distribution among the poorest families of the *mahalas*.

I also became involved with a Romani organization called "Roma Brothers" in Buča Creek. As I had detailed knowledge about size and needs of Roma populations throughout the city, we eventually came to collaborate with other agencies from Tuzla, Visoko, Kakanj, Zenica, and Banja Luka.

Suddenly news about a Romani journalist was spreading throughout the city and beyond. Political activists I had formerly interviewed began to take a greater interest in my work. Soon, I was elected to represent the Roma of Bosnia and Herzegovina in the Union of Yugoslavian Romani Organizations. I was also put in charge of cultural initiatives at the International Romani Union. Though to be sure, I was not letting my day to day work fall by the way side either. I was constantly gathering information for our next broadcast, and worked a great deal even when I was at home.

In those days, I was always sharing my office as many as five or six other journalists. My first office companions were Esad Cerić and Aco Novaković from the news section. I also have fond memories of Stevo Latinović, who edited and hosted international programming. He was always encouraging me to make guest appearances on his program, in order to bring my stories of Romani life to an international audience. Then there was the journalist and poet Alirizah Gaši, always so happy to incorporate my work into the cultural section's programming.

Other happy memories of mine include the poet Velimir Milošević, who was the editor of children's programming at for Radio-TV Sarajevo. He had also encouraged and helped me, and had often told me how important he thought my work was.

I eventually created my own multimedia archives, along with a phone and address books of Romani organizations, businesses, and personalities. Soon thereafter, Radio-Television Sarajevo gave me broad purchasing authority to buy literary works and other materials by and about the Roma.

My newer purchases were added to an already respectable collection of materials I acquired during my travels around Yugoslavia. Many Roma I talked to wanted to do something for their Romani nation, and would give me books they had, along with manuscripts of their own writings; they wanted it all to be used and preserved for the benefit of all Roma.

Unfortunately, like so much else, my archives were lost during the war. I continue to mourn them to this day. They weren't just books, brochures, and music tapes, but also recordings of my radio and television programs as captured by members of my family.

I had strong support from Radio-TV Sarajevo and, like other journalists, I had an unrestricted outgoing line so I could phone and make contacts around the country and abroad. But I still did a lot of my work at home, from developing concepts, to typing up stories and reports, and even making the occasional call. Sometimes my workdays seemed to encompass all 24 hours of the day; and I regularly traveled to Zagreb, Novi Sad, Belgrade, Priština, Skopjeeven, and Tetovo.

In 1990, I travelled to Warsaw, Poland to attend the World Romani Congress. There, I made many contacts with Roma from around the world, and set in motion plans for a concert of Romani music in Vienna, Austria. The event featured musicians from around the world, and I was asked to moderate the discussion segments between performances. Dr. Rajko Đurić helped me a great deal with the preparation of the script.

I got the idea for the concert partly from the smaller scale events we used to organize in Yugoslavia, and partly from observing the growing trend even abroad to organize these sort of humanitarian concerts whenever tragedy struck some group of people or another. Unfortunately only the Roma themselves ever organized such benefit concerts to try to alleviate Romani suffering; nobody else ever noticed my people's misery. I thought it only made sense that I, a journalist acquainted with the harsh realities, should do everything in my power to raise awareness and affect positive change.

*   *   *

Organizing events and benefit concerts wasn't enough for me though. I had the nagging feeling that I could somehow contribute toward better education for Romani children. My own son was growing up quickly, and was already going to school. I always made sure to take time to help him with his studies, and sure enough, he made excellent program.

It was clear to me that if Romani children received more one-on-one instruction to cement both their Romani and their Serbo-Croatian foundations, they would find themselves on more level ground with their classmates. After all, language skills form the foundations of both education and socialization.

I would always do my best to transfer the ideas in my head about teaching onto paper, but it was clear to me that I lacked the educational background to get it quite right. In order to gain that knowledge and understanding, I enrolled in the Pedagogical Academy of Sarajevo. At first, my studies went well enough, but eventually one of my childhood traumas surfaced as a roadblock. I was terrified of water, but the academy's mandatory physical education classes included swimming sessions. The only solution I could find was to transfer to the Pedagogical Academy in Tuzla, where there was no such requirement, and received my degree in 1990.

Even during my studies, I continued to work long hours, partly because I loved my work, and partly because I was paying for my studies myself. After I received my teaching diploma, I gave birth to my second son Zerin. I could have had as much as a year of maternity leave, but I only took three months off in order to nurse my newborn. Once I was able to find a baby sitter, I immediately returned to the station.

During my three months away, Smaragda Klino had substituted for me. She would come to my apartment, and I would help her with the script, the writing, and her Romani pronunciation. Afterwards I would listen to the program and her Romani readings, and would find myself getting annoyed because of all the little details that were not quite the way I wanted them to be. But regardless of that, I really appreciated my colleague's efforts, and recognized that she was quite brave and determined to keep our show going in my absence.

Once I was back behind my microphone, I did my best to maintain a positive work-life balance. I raised my sons according to Romani and Muslim traditions; Edis, my older one, was circumcised at the age of two years, and Zerin, my younger one, just before his seventh month. They also both had their hair cutting rituals, the traditional Romani way of designating the child's godparent. My brave sister Alma was to cut Zerin's first lock of hair, the same way as my father had done for Edis years before.

It is customary to select a child's godfather or godmother from the immediate family, someone with good character, strength, intelligence, sincerity, and good health. My sister Alma, whom I have admired since our childhood for her fearlessness, possessed all of those attributes. She was also resilient and healthy. I wished for my son to have these good qualities of hers when he grew up.

I also did not forget about the Catholic aspects of my upbringing, and we would paint Easter eggs and decorate Christmas Trees without fail. It just felt natural to pass these customs on to my children as well.

Regardless of which religion or tradition each custom originated from, they were all part of my childhood and would now be a part of theirs.

Around that, my colleague Smaragda started taking steps toward setting up a Romani television program, as part of the culturally focused third channel that Radio-TV Sarajevo recently launched. Once the concept gained support, we created a one of program entitled "Malavipe — Encounters".

This new show would be organized along the same general principles as our radio show, but I would occasionally set a theme, such as education, housing issues, social security, or health matters. The format did demand more research on my part, as I not only had to gather enough information to know what to ask our guests, but also had to find pictures and video excerpts to go with our topics. Interviews, special reports, everyday stories, and, of course, music were all part our programming.

"Malavipe — Encounters" was so well received that I was now widely recognized on the street by Roma and non-Roma alike. I enjoyed the special treatment I received at stores, restaurants, and even the hairdresser. Random strangers on the street would suddenly greet me with the words "Lačho djive Romalen", so much so that my colleagues pick-up the habit as their way of gently teasing me.

The recognition felt so wonderful that I didn't even stop to dwell how much effort had gone into getting that far; my sole focus was on what the next steps should be! As positive portrayals of Roma in the media became more prevalent, it seemed to me that our people started to feel freer to openly identify with their Romani nationality.

It was also clear that wherever I went, Roma were proud of my work, and felt I represented them. Thaneh(s)ko Romani women I met would often say, "Here comes our girl!" Many a Romni had told me that they dreamt that their own daughters would one day achieve similar goals. And all Roma simply addressed me as "Derviš's daughter, Dina", which pleased me greatly, for my father was widely respected.

*   *   *

Becoming famous through my work enabled me to help others achieve their own dreams. In fact, I would soon realize that the time had come for me to help my father, who felt ever more Romani with each passing year, accomplish something. Despite being an honest, diligent, hardworking man, he was never able to overcome discrimination in his life. He would always try to envision the path to his goals, and would meticulously plan ahead in order to avoid any dependency on others; because others too often saw him as just a *cigan* and dismissed him, or worse.

These days, whenever he came up with new idea, he would discuss it with me first. As always, he called me at home; never wanting to bother me at work. This time, he wanted to secure a source of income for his old age, for when he was no longer able to drive his taxi. It was an office space for sale in Ciglane, in one of the newer areas of Sarajevo.

Father had money to purchase the space, but he was certain that the seller would refuse him.

"When they see my dark skin, they won't sell me the space," he explained. "They will tell me that it has already been sold, and that I am too late. It all depends, my son, on the connections you have. I have no such connections of my own, just Sarajevan Roma. It is only the peasants that get everything they want."

Father was becoming understandably bitter as he grew older, but thankfully I now had the ability to help him, and the fearless to refuse to back off from any challenge. I knew many people, having made many friends and acquaintances through my work. I decided to take action, and made an offer on the property on my father's behalf.

Even I was not received with open arms. The sellers just kept asking for more and more documents and paperwork. New problems would constantly surface even before the old ones got resolved. But I was determined to purchase. Though it took me months to gather the required papers, some of it only thanks to the connections I had made through Radio-TV Sarajevo. In the end though, I triumphed. It may have only been because of my stubbornness and my fame, but I had gotten my father his office space.

*   *   *

Around that same time, the city began implementing its long planned project of moving Roma out of Gorica to make way for commercial

Our house in Gorica

development. Gorica's Roma were given apartments in different parts
of the city. This meant both that they had to abandon the houses
they had been living in for generations, and also that they would
find themselves dispersed and living among strangers in their new
dwellings. Father didn't wait until he was arbitrarily assigned a new
home; instead, he moved into a vacant apartment in Ciglane, on the
same street as his newly purchased office space. He, mother, and Alin
all left the Tahirović family home to move into this apartment on Mitar
Trifunović Učo Street, nowadays called Dajanli Ibrahimbega street.
But after some time, it became clear that the city's plan was going
nowhere fast, and sooon enough father and mother stopped spending
much time in the new apartment, and instead we would continue to
find them back in our old family home in our Gorica *mahala*, at 35
Dajanli Osmanbega street.

Thanks to my still being registered as living in the basement, Father
was entitled to an additional bachelor apartment on top of the one
he already got. As he already had a place for him, mother, and Alin;
he immediately signed over this apartment to me. He was always

thinking of me. I saw this bachelor apartment as a very special gift from him, a sign of his love, care, and esteem for me.

This love that my father and I had for one another, tied us together. Roma would often call me "Daughter of our Derviš", and sometimes they would even call him "Derviš, father of our Dina Tahirović Sijerčić". They saw that I was one of their own, and, like my father, they saw that I was a Romni who had made it in this world. This knowledge filled them, like my father, with satisfaction. And I was satisfied as well, secure in the knowledge that this was only my first step on the long road toward conscious living.

I was now juggling a steadily increasing number of responsibilities both at work and at home, and even had the beginnings of an idea to start a school for Romani children, where they would receive the individual attention I knew they needed. And perhaps because I was so taken up with what was happening in my own life and my immediate community, I wasn't seeing the events unfolding more widely around us. Perhaps I just want to acknowledge the nationalistic ideas that were slowly taking hold of people's minds, slowly changing their characters, and even their faces.

*   *   *

I had become financially well off, but never forgot about dear Behara, the old Romni who had taught me that we go into the next life with nothing, regardless of whether in this one we were rich or poor. Whenever I visited Ilidža, I would go and visit her. I don't know what kind of respect wealthy Nail received from his people, but I knew that impoverished Behara was the eldest in her community, and was the "ceribaša" of her *čerga,* and her people called her "phuridej", "old mother". Her words and decisions were respected and obeyed by all. Everyone would ask for advice, as she was the one that organized the community's everyday life. Behara decided who would beg at which location, who would tell fortunes, who would fetch wood or water, and who would go to the city for the day. She was a courageous woman whose old age didn't prevent her from fulfilling her duties.

It was in her demeanor that I first caught hints of the alarming changes happening throughout Yugoslavia. She ceased to seem peaceful, and instead appeared lost and paranoid, as if she was expecting somebody or something. She would twitch when hearing a loud voice or a baby's cry. She stopped looking like a resilient Ceribaša Romni, and instead had the appearance of a frightened old woman.

I asked her what was happening in her life, whether there was somebody threatening her? She would turn around her, and in a soft voice, she would confide to me, "Those living around us constantly curse our *"Cigan* mothers". They attack us, and want to chase us out of here. My son, something is being stirred around here." Even as she explained these things to me, she was careful to try to appear calm, lest anybody guess what she was talking about. Only rarely, in occasional unguarded moments would she would roll her eyes, widened by fear, while tightening up her lips.

"I hope it won't be like the last time during World War II," she whispered. "After the war, only the animals, birds, dogs, and ants remembered our dead. We also spoke about them when amongst our own kind, but others never did. Everybody else spoke about their own victims, only we never talked publicly about ours. And if we had, who would have listened to us? They didn't care. It was as if we didn't exist. During World War II, we were all on the list for concentration camps. Very few people escaped that tragic destiny."

I knew what she was talking about, and what she was afraid of, my dear Behara. She talked about the suffering of our people during the war; about the concentration camps where our people were murdered just for being Roma. This woman, normally stronger than most men, was giving way to fear in the face of the rising powers whose roars grew louder everyday throughout Yugoslavia.

My grandmother Mejra's parents had perished in a concentration camp without leaving a trace; nobody even bothered to record their names. I remembered some books from Romani authors who dared to write the truth of what had been done to our people. But most non-Roma didn't believe that it was important to include our innocent victims in their totals. In the Ustaše's so-called Independent State of Croatia, specifically at Jasenovac camp, recorded 10,000 Roma victims. But the recorded names represented only a tenth of our dead

Further research has shown that between 80,000 and 100,000 Roma perished in Jasenovac alone between 1941 and 1945. But we never learned this in school, as our victims were mentioned only in passing. Dead Roma were not really counted, as Bahara often said. The same situation seems like in the rest of the countries that were under Fascist rule. There were many assumptions, but few exact numbers. In 1996, my acquaintance and colleague Dragoljub Acković had published a book entitled "Ašunen Romalen" through Rrominterpress of Radio B92. Therein, he wrote: "In my opinion, about 3 million Roma perished in this cataclysm. My research is in accordance with claims made by international research that claims there were 3 million and 62 thousand Roma victims in World War II."

But these facts were rarely discussed by anyone except us Roma. And even we seldom spoke about it, as it was something everyone wished to forget. Repeating that we lived and still live under the same blue sky was futile. A time of evil was upon us again, and we were once more unwelcome in the only world we had ever known as our own.

Behara remembered the old days, and the memories caused her much distress. She was afraid, and passed her fears onto me as well. One day, when I entered her house, she closed the door so no one could hear us or see us. She raised her long skirt, revealing another one underneath, as well as long underpants, and a cloth bag tied around her tiny waist. She pulled out a gun, and said to me "Dikh gova jagalo!" I understood what she meant. "If they come, I will get rid of them."

She told me that our people had a way of foreseeing impending misfortune, as though through some sort of sixth sense. I guess it's a gift from God. It's all the protection we have. Since then, I've come to feel that I too possess this power.

When she had pulled out that gun, she showed me how she would fire it. For that brief moment, she believed that she could somehow defend herself and her home. Then, she remembered reality, and that others had mightier weapons than hers; ones that could bring destruction even before she'd have a chance to even draw.

"I fear for our people. If they kill me, my suffering ends there and then. But if they kill our children, they put the very life and future of our nation in jeopardy. They could easily enter into our *čerga* and exterminate us all. We have no protection. That tiny pistol of mine can only save one person. You should run also, my son, while there is still time. *Amen musaj te nashaven ande Italija!*"

Suddenly, she pulled me towards her, happy for having figured it out, and decided she would save her čerga at this very moment. She kissed me on the forehead, and said, "Hajde ach Devleha!" I whispered back, "Hajde dza Devleha, mi Behara!" and left with tears in my eyes.

Behara correctly sensed that her pistol would be no defense against those who would wish her people harm. She decided to move her people out, and flee to Italy before it was too late. I, however, still believed in miracles, and hoped that the evils of the past would not be repeated.

Soon, I started feeling the threat that Behara had already decided to flee. After our TV show's 1992's Romani New Year celebrations, we received criticisms of a sort I still don't fully understand. It started with an article written by my old high school teacher, the man who had first encouraged me toward journalism, the man who had welcomed me to Radio-TV Sarajevo.

He questioned and attacked the station's politics along with our programming. He questioned why Roma were allotted television time for their New Year celebrations, and claimed that we "cigani" soiled the respectable Serbian celebrations appropriate for the season. He claimed Radio-TV Sarajevo's provocative priorities were designed to deprive Serbs of media time and even their national rights.

After that article appeared, our television show was immediately cancelled. Though our radio show continued to air until we fled the city, in hindsight it was obviously the beginning of the end.

Departure

Though our television show had been canceled following the attacks of my former teacher, I still carried hope. I continued to work on my radio program, continued to record and broadcast, certain that other opportunities would arise sooner or later. We regular citizens of all backgrounds, accustomed to living together peacefully, couldn't imagine that it was our togetherness that would become the target of nationalists on all sides. We naïvely believed that no one would hurt us, simply because we ourselves hadn't done anything to offend anyone. We just wanted to continue to live and work together as Yugoslavians—all different, but all equal.

Even after barricades started showing up throughout the city and shootings started to become commonplace, I, as many others, continued to go to work every day. I continued to enjoy my streetcar rides, and continued to take pleasure in watching life in the city unfold every morning. I would try to plan my day ahead, how to organize events, who to call, where to go.

But my once beloved office was already a very different place. Yesterday's friends, who had once supported me, now looked at me as though I were an enemy. They would not even try to hide their animosity. With every irritable glance and angry gaze, they would let me know that I didn't belong, that my services were no longer wanted.

Even the leadership was in constant turmoil. Editors separated into factions according to their nationalities: Serbian, Croatian, and Bosniak. And if that wasn't enough, they struggled to imprint the same divisions on all the station's shows. Nobody asked for my opinions anymore, though I was still the Editor-in-chief of the "Lačho djive, Romalen" with a team of 5 - 6 collaborators. But Romani programming no longer mattered to anyone. The new politics that now dominated the country had no use for minority programming. Instead, the growing political divisions found their way into every news broadcast, program, and editorial.

The Yugoslav spirit we had all once believed in was suddenly vanishing into the mist. Those of us who still believed in it no longer mattered. Everything was now viewed through the tainting lenses of nationalism, and I had an increasingly hard time coping with it all. Going to work was steadily becoming a torture, and the pleasure of my morning trips was now only a distant memory.

In previous years, spring would always bring a burst of new energy into the city, as people would rejoice the passing of the harsh, smog-filled Sarajevan winter. The plants in the parks would start budding, and the breeze would descend from the mountain tops, bringing the whole city which alive. We would inhale with deep breaths the new scents spreading from Bembaša to Ilidža. But this time, spring brought only the stench of gunpowder and burnt buildings. Each day we could hear more and more gun shots echoing through the city, and news about killings was spreading quickly. Everyone was expecting the worst in that April of 1992. Even Sarajevo's decades of peace and cosmopolitanism couldn't stop the advancing snipers from the mountains or their shells. Sarajevans were being killed on the streets daily. It looked more like a horror movie than real life, but we couldn't just walk out from the movie theater. We had no choice but to stay, and wait to see whether our bullet would hit or miss.

Everything looked the same, from the bank in Tito street to the Alipaša field, where the Radio-TV Sarajevo building was located, and every few hundred meters, men in uniforms were carrying riffles.

The city's entire character changed, and uniformed men carrying rifles marched every few hundred meters. The uniforms were unrecognizable, as each group wore a different one. I had no idea whose military was patrolling Sarajevo, and could not begin to guess who appointed them and whom they were here to protect

The filth in the air and the suffocating atmosphere of the city were choking me. I didn't have to work anymore in the office, and I could no longer travel safely throughout the city. Nobody cared about the fate of Roma anymore. I had a hard time accepting the loss of the job that I loved so much, but I decided to take an unpaid leave of absence to look after my children. With snipers shooting from hiding places all over the city, each egress onto the streets could turn out to be the last one. My older son was constantly running around outside despite my prohibitions, as he just couldn't stand being confined to the house.

Then our telephone lines went dead, leaving us feeling more isolated and alone than ever before. The Serbian militia along with what used to be the national army showered the Baščaršija and the city centre with grenades. Throughout that attack we stayed in the basement shelters.

We had very little food left at home. I thought more and more often about Behara and her pistol. We were completely defenseless. Even if there were ten such pistols to each remaining neighbour, we would have still been powerless against the forces that were closing in on us. Behara had decided to flee with her people after spending so many years in one place. She remembered the fate of the Roma during World War II, and wanted to save the children. Why did I not think of that sooner?

My feelings of guilt only increased with my claustrophobia. In the basement, I felt like I was in some earthly hell, and I was constantly choking from the dust. My children held on to me tightly. When one explosion sounded like it had been particularly close, my older son

Edis grabbed my leg, and whispered, "Mom, I'm afraid!" I watched his young face, distorted with fear; and could barely recognize my son's beautiful face.

I held him close to me, and in that moment I decided to act. I had to save my children. The only thing we could do was to leave the city. In that basement, I could only cry with them, pray to God for help, and wait to either die from hunger or one of the grenades.

Behara, the woman ceribaša from the Romani *mahala* had fled with her people towards Italy. My sister Alma was also staying in Italy by that time, and my other sister, Elvira, was living in Germany. With my sons clinging on to me in fear, I decided that we would also go abroad. We would find a country that was merciful to refugees. My parents didn't want to leave the country. "Where? Who would take us? And how will we make living?", they would ask. This was their city, where they had lived all their lives. They could not imagine a new life abroad worth living.

My husband, my children, and I, packed with the bare essentials, managed to find seats on a bus that was leaving the city. The Serbs allowed buses carrying refugees to leave the city. Maybe they wanted us all gone so there would no one left to defend it from their forces...

Once we left the city, we became refugees. How many more times I would hear that word throughout my life! In Bosnian, Romani, German, and English; Našavdo, Muhadžir, Flüchting, Refugee: a stranger abroad, forever at the mercy of foreigners.

The war had thus interrupted my life and my dreams. Though almost two decades had passed since then, the sort of progressive Romani programming that our shows had featured never reappeared to this day. And neither I, nor my Romani nation has ever fully healed from the hateful brutality that brought everything undone.

E ZHIVINDI YAG
THE LIVING FIRE

BY RONALD LEE

Ronald Lee's autobiographical novel, formerly published as "Goddam Gypsy", is an intense, fast moving, and brutally honest affair.

Yanko—a Canadian Rom who 'took the non-Romani way but didn't go far'—seeks his fortunes both among and apart from the Roma, never quite finding his place. His story exposes the out of sight, out of mind world of Canada's Roma in 1970's Montréal: Parties, rackets, bar brawls, weddings, desperate poverty, and intermittent police raids fuel in Yanko the passion, creativity, and rebellious defiance that is The Living Fire.

MAGORIA BOOKS
www.MagoriaBooks.com

DUKH — PAIN

BY HEDINA TAHIROVIĆ SIJERČIĆ

Hedina Tahirović Sijerčić's collection of richly evocative poems weave together the author's fleeting joys and enduring tragedies with traditional Romani folklore.

Hedina's poetry is enlightening in its candidness, which shatters the fanciful myth of the mysterious and ever-carefree Roma, replacing it with lyric images of a people living, loving, and dying, not immune to the caprice of the world that surrounds them. It is through such tragedies that the lingering message of these poems has become simply dukh, pain.

RROMANE PARAMICHA:
Stories and Legends of the Gurbeti Roma

BY HEDINA TAHIROVIĆ SIJERČIĆ

Rromane Paramicha is a unique collection of folktales and legends that bring alive the rich cultural and religious traditions of the Roma. Hedina Tahirović Sijerčić, internationally published Romani poet and author, offers us the stories from her childhood with the authenticity of a direct inheritor of oral tradition. This special bilingual edition contains both faithful English translations, as well as the Gurbeti Romani originals of each story, with a selection of Doris Greven's beautiful watercolour illustrations.

Visit www.RomaniFolktales.com for more information.

MAGORIA BOOKS
www.MagoriaBooks.com

Also from
MAGORIA BOOKS

ROMANI FOLKTALES
(illustrated children's books)

BY HEDINA TAHIROVIĆ SIJERČIĆ

A series of beautifully illustrated children's books featuring excerpted Romani folktales from "Rromane Paramicha: Stories and Legends of the Gurbeti Roma".

In each book, Hedina Tahirović Sijerčić, internationally published Romani Poet and Author, brings us the stories from her childhood with the vivid watercolour painted illustrations of Doris Greven. These special bilingual editions contain both the English versions and the Romani originals of each story.

Visit www.RomaniFolktales.com for more information.

MAGORIA BOOKS
www.MagoriaBooks.com

ROMANI DICTIONARY
(Kalderash – English)

BY RONALD LEE

As Ian Hancock notes in the introduction, this dictionary has been years in the making, and its early drafts have been in circulation among a select few for at least three decades. It should come as no surprise then that this Kalderash dictionary, by Learn Romani author Ronald Lee, is fundamentally different from many previously published Romani dictionaries: Firstly, it is compiled by a native Romani speaker; secondly, it covers and, where appropriate, differentiates European and North American Kalderash terms; and thirdly, it is a decidedly academic quality work that does not shy away from Romani grammar. Prefaced by a grammatical primer, containing over 12,000 lexical items, and filled with countless real world examples of idiomatic usage, this book is an indispensable resource for anyone looking to learn or work with Kalderash Romani.

MAGORIA BOOKS
www.MagoriaBooks.com

ROMANI DICTIONARY
(Gurbeti – English / English – Gurbeti)

BY HEDINA TAHIROVIĆ SIJERČIĆ

A comprehensive bi-directional dictionary of the compiler's native Gurbeti Romani dialect, with both grammatical classification and many examples of real-world usage. Ideal for both practical use by native speakers and language learners, as well as for academics interested in lexical comparisons of Romani dialects.

Spoken by large groups of Roma still living in the successor states of the former Yugoslavia, as well as the widely emigrated diaspora created by the turbulent history of the region; Gurbeti Romani is the native language of many a Romani artist and writer, and thus the dialect used in several notable books, Hedina Tahirović Sijerčić's numerous titles among them.

MAGORIA BOOKS
www.MagoriaBooks.com

ME NI DŽANAV TE KAMAV
(tentative title)

BY RUŽDIJA SEJDOVIĆ

Ruždija Sejdović's intimate and symbolically charged love poems bring into keen focus the passion and suffering of both the poet and his people. The delicately crafted verses shift imperceptably from speaking with the voice of one man to echoing the cries of a rising Romani nation still haunted by European demons.

Containing the author's poems in English and Hungarian in addition to the original Romani; this book aims to be a mirror for and a bridge between peoples both kindred and other.

MAGORIA BOOKS
www.MagoriaBooks.com

About Magoria Books

Magoria Books is an independent international publisher of Romani books. Our aim is to provide Romani authors with opportunities to continue to develop and enrich the ever-growing body of Romani literature, and also to raise the profile and positive depictions of Roma and Romani culture around the world.

We therefore encourage Romani poets, writers, and activists to approach us with their ideas and proposals. We are particularly interested in folktales, poetry, and other culturally focused manuscripts, including those written in Romani or Central/East European languages.

We are also interested in partnerships with translators, community organizations, and foreign publishers to find ways to increase distribution, availability, and impact of both existing and upcoming titles.

Write to us at:

publisher@magoriabooks.com